The Campaigns of the Coldstream Guards, 1793-1815

The Campaigns of the Coldstream Guards, 1793-1815

The Revolutionary War, Peninsular War and
Waterloo Described by an Eyewitness Officer

ILLUSTRATED

Daniel Mackinnon

LEONAUR

The Campaigns of the Coldstream Guards, 1793-1815
The Revolutionary War, Peninsular War and Waterloo Described by an Eyewitness Officer
by Daniel Mackinnon

ILLUSTRATED

FIRST EDITION

Leonaur is an imprint of Oakpast Ltd

Copyright in this form © 2021 Oakpast Ltd

ISBN: 978-1-78282-958-4 (hardcover)
ISBN: 978-1-78282-959-1 (softcover)

http://www.leonaur.com

Publisher's Notes

Contents

CHAPTER 1

First Batallions Embark for Holland

On the eventful murder of Louis the Sixteenth, Jan. 21st, 1793, England declared war, and joined the confederacy formed against the regicide government of France.

The first battalions of the three regiments of Guards received orders to prepare for embarkation, and all their companies were completed. (To four sergeants, four corporals, and two drummers.) The grenadiers were formed into a separate battalion under Colonel Leigh of the Third Guards, and Major-General Lake was appointed (Feb. 24th) to command the brigade.

Previous to their departure (Feb. 25th) they were inspected by his Majesty King George the Third. From the parade they marched to Greenwich, where their embarkation was witnessed by the Royal Family. After anchoring at the Nore, the convoy sailed for Helvoetsluys; on landing, (May 3rd) the troops were placed in *schuyts* and sent to Dort.

The Prussian troops were advancing by Bois-le-Duc, while a corresponding movement was made by the Hanoverians, who had been joined by the British under the Duke of York.

At Dort, a light company was formed from the brigade of Guards, and attached to the grenadier battalion, which now consisted of five companies under Lieutenant-Colonel James Perrin of the First Guards. The Guards embarked for Bergen-op-Zoom on the first of April, at which place they were quartered some days; thence they proceeded by the canal through Antwerp and Ghent, and on the nineteenth landed at Bruges. They afterwards marched through Thielt, Courtray, and Tournay, and reached the village of Orcq on the twenty-fifth.

Two light companies were formed at home and added to the establishment of the regiment under a warrant dated nineteenth of April.

******

George Rex.—Whereas we have been pleased to direct that our Coldstream regiment of Foot Guards under your command shall be forthwith augmented with two light-infantry companies, each to consist of 4 sergeants, 4 corporals, 2 drummers, and 71 private men, besides commissioned officers; These are to authorise you, by beat of drum or otherwise, to raise so many men in any county or part of our kingdom of Great Britain, as shall be wanted to complete the said augmentation. And all magistrates, justices of the peace, constables, and other our civil officers whom it may concern, are hereby required to be assisting unto you in providing quarters, impressing carriages, and otherwise as there shall be occasion, Given at our Court at St. James's, this 19th day of April, 1793, in the 33rd year of our reign.

By His Majesty's command,

George Yonge.

To our most dearly beloved son and councillor, Frederick Duke of York, General in our army, and Colonel of our Coldstream regiment of Foot Guards, or to the officer appointed by him to raise men for our said regiment.

(Placed on the establishment from 25th June, 1793.)

******

A great deal of skirmishing, and some sharp affairs had taken place between the armies, previous to the arrival of the brigade of Guards.

In consequence of General Dampierre's repeated attacks, in May on the Prussians, the Guards were greatly harassed, and constantly kept under arms in readiness to move. At midnight, on the seventh, they left their cantonments at Orcq, near Tournay, and proceeded to the camp of Maulde, where they halted at daylight, and joined the Austrian and Prussian infantry; the former were ordered to dislodge the enemy from St. Amand, and also to drive them from the wood. In the afternoon the Duke of York marched through St. Amand, which place had been obstinately maintained, as appeared from the ruined and dilapidated state of the buildings and the dead lying in all directions. The Coldstream Guards advanced to the forest, where they halted till the arrival of the Prussian General Knobelsdorf, who rode up, and, with a smile, said in broken English, that:

He had reserved for the Coldstream Guards the honour, the

special glory of dislodging the French from their intrenchments in the forest, that the British troops need only show themselves in the wood, and the French would retire.

He however omitted to state, that the Austrians had been three times successively repulsed, with the loss of one thousand seven hundred men, and General Knobelsdorf proposed for the Coldstream the honour of performing with six hundred rank and file what five thousand Austrians had not been able to accomplish. The fact was, that on the failure of the Austrians, application had been made to General Knobelsdorf for some fresh battalions from the Prussian Army, which requisition he immediately made over to the Duke of York. The Coldstream, under Colonel Pennington, was moved towards the wood of Vicogne, the Prussian general accompanying them himself along the *chaussée*. On arriving at the skirts of the wood, he pointed to the entrance and galloped off.

The enemy's redoubts commanded the *chaussée* leading to the wood of St. Amand, and on the approach of the right companies of the Coldstream, who had nearly closed on the flying enemy, a tremendous fire was opened within pistol-shot by guns wheeled from a battery concealed in the bushes and underwood of the forest. On passing a temporary bridge over a broad ditch, the two right companies under Colonels Bosville and Gascoyne lost, in ten minutes, more than half their numbers, and retired to the skirt of the wood. So sudden was their onset that the last division had scarcely crossed the hedge-row, separating the *chaussée* from the wood, when the two leading companies found themselves under a destructive fire. The left wing did not lose a man.

In this action the French general, Dampierre, lost his thigh by a cannon-ball, and died next day. Ensign Howard of the Coldstream, who carried the colours, the sergeant-major, two sergeants, and seventy-three rank and file were killed, wounded, or missing.

★★★★★★

The sergeant-major of the Coldstream regiment, by name Darley, was amongst the wounded in the action of the 8th.

He performed prodigies of valour; he had his arm broke and shattered by a ball, but yet continued to fight with the most animated and determined bravery for near two hours. He put to death a French officer who made an attack upon him, but at length had his leg broke by another cannon shot, in consequence of which he fell into the hands of the French.

The Duke of York sent a trumpeter on the morning of the 9th, to say that the surgeon who attended him should be liberally rewarded for his trouble, and to request that no expense should be spared in procuring him every comfort that his situation would admit of.

The following letter was written by Captain Hewgill of the Coldstream, and Secretary to His Royal Highness, to Sergeant-Major Coleman of the battalion of the Coldstream here:

Headquarters, May 10, Tournay.

Sergeant-Major Coleman,

I write to you by desire of His Royal Highness the Duke of York to acquaint you, for the information of Mrs. Darley, that her husband is alive, and, though in custody of the enemy, has written a few lines to say he is well treated and taken care of. The duke feels much for his unfortunate situation, and has given orders that a trumpeter shall be sent tomorrow to him with whatever he wants, and a letter to acquaint the French surgeon attending him that he will pay all the expenses of his cure.

He has one arm and his thigh broke, besides two other wounds: there may therefore be some doubt of his recovery, which I think you should take an opportunity of communicating to your daughter.

His Royal Highness, as well as every officer and soldier of the Coldstream, can bear witness to his good conduct and gallantry in the action of the 8th.

Brave as a lion, he fought with his broken arm till a second shot brought him to the ground; and since his confinement he has dictated a letter, wherein he explains his money concerns with an incredible degree of accuracy and honesty.

In short, all our prayers attend this valuable man, and I have authority to say from the commander-in-chief that he will never forget him.   E. Hewgill,

(*European Magazine*, 1793, page 395.)

★★★★★★

The conduct of the Coldstream was thus noticed in a letter written by the adjutant-general, to the forces under the Duke of York, Colonel Sir James Murray, dated the tenth of May.

The attack commenced about seven o'clock. It was directed

against the posts occupied by General Clairfait, which extend from the Scheld to the Abbaye de Vicogne, and the Prussian corps which defends the wood in the front of the high-road, leading from that place to St. Amand.

To these points were directed the whole efforts of the French Army, which had been previously reinforced by all they could bring together from every quarter, General Knobelsdorf having been under the necessity of sending a considerable part of his troops to support the Austrians at the Abbaye de Vicogne, His Royal Highness about five o'clock left two battalions in the camp at Maulde, and marched with the Coldstream, the flank battalion, and that of the Third regiment, to his support. When the battalion of the Coldstream, which was upon the left, arrived, the enemy had nearly reached the road; they already commanded it to a great degree by their fire: the guns attached to the battalion were placed upon it, and, by a well-directed and well-supported fire, kept the battery which was opposed to them in check, and did considerable execution.

The battalion advanced into the wood, attacked and drove the enemy before them; in going forward they became unfortunately opposed to the fire of a battery, from which they suffered severely. They fell back to their position at the edge of the wood, which they maintained for the rest of the day, notwithstanding a heavy cannonade. The enemy made no attempt to approach them. Nothing can exceed the spirit and bravery displayed by the men and officers of the battalion upon this occasion.

On the eleventh of May the following General Order was issued:—

Headquarters Tournay,
His Royal Highness the Duke of York returns his warmest thanks to the officers and privates who were engaged on the eighth instant, and particularly to those of the Coldstream Guards, who bore the brunt of the attack. The Hanoverians to relieve the brigade of Guards in all their posts tomorrow, in order to ease those troops who have undergone so much fatigue. (On the twelfth of May a *feu-de-joie* was fired in celebration of the victory.)

Condé was now blockaded; and previous to the investment of Valenciennes, it was necessary to attack the fortified camp of Famars.

On the twenty-third of May the Duke of York led the first column, consisting of sixteen battalions of English, with some Hanoverian and Austrian troops. After a cannonade, the hussars crossed the Roxelle, without opposition, at the village of Mershe, and on the advance of a body of infantry, which would have turned the batteries, the enemy retreated to a redoubt they had constructed behind the village of Famars. General Clairfait also attacked the French stationed on the heights of Auzain, which were obstinately defended; but at length the Austrians gained the post. This success enabled the Prince of Cobourg to complete the investment of Valenciennes; the camp of Famars being occupied by the English and Hanoverians. The redoubt behind Famars was held till flight, when the enemy abandoned it and retired across the Scheldt

The siege of Valenciennes was entrusted to the Duke of York, who carried it on with great vigour.

★★★★★★

About ten o'clock, on the night of the 2nd of June, a working party of the Guards, and the brigade of the line, consisting of about 300 men, and a strong covering party under the engineer, began the entrenchments, July the 3rd, the Earl of Cavan was wounded in the head by a piece of shell. On the 9th a soldier of the Coldstream was killed by a shell in the trenches. 12th of July, one of the Coldstream was dangerously wounded by a shell. 18th, four men were wounded by a shell. On the 25th the first mine was sprung, then a second and third within the space of a few minutes; after the third mine was sprung, the troops, being in readiness, rushed with the greatest impetuosity and jumped over the *palisadoes*, carrying all before them at the point of the bayonet the enemy, after a stout resistance, left the works in possession of the victors.—*Extract from the Journal of Corporal Robert Brown of the Coldstream Guards.*

★★★★★★

After a practicable breach was effected, (July 25th), the duke ordered the English and Austrians to make a general assault: the storming party consisted of one hundred and fifty men of the Guards, and the same number from the line, under Major-General Abercrombie: they succeeded and carried the outworks.

★★★★★★

On the twenty-sixth of July the following general order was issued:—His Royal Highness the Commander-in-Chief returns his thanks to Major-General Abercrombie, Colonel Leigh, and

Lieutenant-Colonel Doyle, for the gallantry they showed on the attack last night.

★★★★★★

The loss in the battalion companies of the Coldstream during the siege was two rank and file killed; one captain (Earl of Cavan), one sergeant, thirteen rank and file, wounded; one rank and file died of his wounds. The flank battalion lost four rank and file killed; two sergeants, eighteen rank and file, wounded: three rank and file died afterwards. The town capitulated on the twenty-eighth, and was taken possession of by the Duke of York, in the name of the Emperor of Germany: this political error rallied into unanimity the hitherto hesitating inclinations of the French people. A detachment of the Guards occupied the gate of Cambray.

Condé had already surrendered, and the garrison were made prisoners of war, after a siege of three months, during which they had been much reduced by famine and disease.

On the twenty-ninth a reinforcement of about six hundred men under Lieutenant-Colonel Tad Watson of the Third Guards joined the brigade; amongst them were three light infantry companies, one for each of the regiments of Guards: the company belonging to the First regiment was commanded by Lieutenant-Colonel Ludlow, that of the Coldstream by Lieutenant-Colonel Eld, and that of the Third Guards by Lieutenant-Colonel Campbell; these companies joined the flank battalion, and completed it to eight companies.

The flank companies of the Guards and light infantry, with the men who had composed the storming party on the twenty-fifth instant lined the road from the Cambray gate to Briquet, when the garrison of Valenciennes marched out for the purpose of laying down their arms.

On the sixth of August the Coldstream proceeded towards Cambray, and encamped about two leagues to the eastward of that fortress. Some days after the Austrians had taken possession of Valenciennes the French were obliged to quit their strong position behind the Scheld; and Cambray was summoned.

★★★★★★

It was reported in Paris that Cambray had been summoned to surrender on the 8th by General Boros, and that the *commandant* returned the following answer:

I have received your letter, general, and have no other answer to return than that I know not how to surrender, but I know how to fight.—National Convention, Aug. 16. Declay,

******

At a council of war, it was agreed, in opposition to the opinion of the Prince of Cobourg and of General Clairfait, that the army under the Duke of York should separate from the Austrians. The British, in consequence, broke up, and marched on the fourteenth of August on their route to Dunkirk, the siege of that fortress having been determined on for the purpose of replacing it under the dominion of England. The Guards passed Tournay on the fifteenth, Lannoy on the sixteenth, and halted next day, with the exception of the flank battalion, which encamped near a village called Ghelins. On the eighteenth His Royal Highness proceeded from Turcoin to Menin.

The French had driven the Dutch troops from Lincelles, which they had occupied by an order from the Prince of Orange. Major-General Lake was directed, with three battalions, consisting of the First, Coldstream, and Third Guards, to assist the Dutch troops in recapturing that place; but the latter had retreated by a different road from that taken by the Guards in their advance.

******

General Lake had despatched an *aide-de-camp* to the headquarters of His Royal Highness the Commander-in-Chief at Menin, informing him of the flight of the Dutch, and the perilous situation of the Guards; the Second Brigade, as well as some battalions of Hessians, were consequently ordered to support them; but could not possibly arrive till the affair was terminated. The Dutch troops having been also ordered to reoccupy their former position, the Guards were permitted to march back to their camp, and the redoubts having been levelled with the ground, the post was early the next morning abandoned as untenable, being only two leagues and a half distant (above seven miles and a half from Lisle.)

The Dutch were so thoroughly ashamed of their behaviour, and so crestfallen, that they slunk about, avoiding as much as possible the British soldiers; and the Prince of Waldeck, who commanded the garrison of Menin, the next morning, in a very noble manner, caught the first officer of the Guards he met with by the hand, and after extolling the gallantry of the British soldiers (when surrounded by his own officers,) exclaimed, "Your glory is our shame."—*Campaign of 1793, 1794 and Retreat through Holland to Westphalia*, vol. i.

★★★★★★

Notwithstanding this circumstance, and the decided superiority on the part of the enemy, Lake made his preparations, and formed under a heavy fire, when he attacked a redoubt of unusual size and strength, situated on high ground in front of Lincelles. The woods were strongly defended by the enemy, and their flanks were covered by ditches. The column was led by the First Guards, which deployed with great celerity, the Coldstream forming on the left. The line then advanced amidst a shower of grape, and after two volleys made a furious charge, accompanied by loud huzzas, stormed the works, and dispersed the enemy, who vainly attempted to rally.

★★★★★★

"The French, who had been accustomed to the cold, lifeless attacks of the Dutch, were amazed at the spirit and intrepidity of the British, and not much relishing the manner of our salute immediately gave way, abandoning all that was in the place, and, in their flight, threw away both arms and accoutrements. We took one stand of colours, two pieces of cannon, with two pieces they had taken from the Dutch."—*Journal of Corporal Robert Brown of the Coldstream Guards.*

The adjutant-general in his dispatch, says, "The battalions were instantly formed, and advanced under a heavy fire, with an order and intrepidity, for which no praise can be too high. After firing three or four rounds they rushed on with their bayonets. The enemy amounted to about five thousand men, and lost eleven guns and about three hundred men."

★★★★★★

At ten o'clock p.m. (Aug. 18th), the pursuit was discontinued, when the Fourteenth and Fifty-Third regiments with some Hessian infantry relieved the Guards, who returned to their former ground near Menin, where they arrived, after undergoing great fatigue, about three o'clock in the morning.

In this action the Coldstream lost Lieutenant-Colonel Bosville, and eight rank and file killed. Lieutenant-Colonel Gascoyne, Ensign Bayly, two sergeants, and forty-five rank and file were wounded.

★★★★★★

It is said that Lieutenant-Colonel Bosville's death was in consequence of his extraordinary height, being six feet four inches high: he was shot in the forehead.

Three hundred and forty-six rank, and file of the Coldstream

15

were engaged on the 18th of August, 1793.

★★★★★★

The following order appeared on the nineteenth of August:—

His Royal Highness the Commander-in-Chief returns his warmest thanks to Major-General Lake, Colonels Hulse, Greenfield, Pennington, Major Wright, and the officers and men belonging to the brigade of Guards and artillery under his command, for the gallantry and intrepidity they so evidently showed in the attack of the French redoubts at the village of Lincelles yesterday afternoon."

On the twentieth the Guards passed through Ypres, and encamped next day near Furnes; from whence the Duke of York proceeded on the twenty-second in pursuit of the enemy to Ghievelde: on his approach they abandoned their position, and His Royal Highness was enabled at once to take up the ground which he intended to occupy during the siege of Dunkirk. The Guards encamped to the left of the canal, the flank battalion on the right.

A general attack was made on the outposts between the canal of Furnes and the sea. (Aug. 24th). The flank battalion forced their way through deep ditches full of water, and strong double hedges, driving the enemy into the town,

Among the killed was Lieutenant-Colonel Eld of the light company of the Coldstream, with eight rank and file: one lieutenant, twenty-five rank and file, were wounded.

The Hanoverians, meanwhile, under Marshal Freytag, with an army of observation of twelve thousand men, kept in awe the garrison of Bergnes and the camp at Mont-Cassel.

When the committee of public safety heard of the separation of the Duke of York's army from the Austrians, they lost no time in sending Generals Souham and Hoche with fresh troops to the assistance of Dunkirk

O'Moran, a supposed spy, was seized by the orders of Hoche, and sent to Paris.

★★★★★★

O'Moran was supposed to keep up a treasonable correspondence with the British, as will be seen by the following extract of a letter from General Hoche to the War Department:—

"*Je suis arrivé ici avec le Général Souham, qui est un vrai sans-culutte. Enfin, à force de travail, nous commençons à nous reconnoitre. Pitt avait ici des agens, Des papiers incendiaires ont été répandus, des signaux donnés à la flotte ennemie, mouillée à trois quarts de lieue de la ville,*

*et les matelots, frappés d'une terreur panique, et probablement travaillés
par l'aristocratie, s'étaieiit insurgés."*

★★★★★★

On the evening of the sixth of September, the enemy made a sortie
from Dunkirk, their attack was principally directed against the right,
but was gallantly sustained by the First Brigade: the Fourteenth regiment suffered severely.

Houchard had arrived with strong reinforcements for the relief of
Dunkirk: he attacked Freytag's position, by whom a partial retreat was
effected. The following day the attack was renewed, and General Walmoden was obliged to give way, with the loss of three hundred men
and three guns. In this action His Royal Highness Prince Adolphus,
since Duke of Cambridge, and Marshal Freytag were wounded, and
for a short time made prisoners.

The loss of the Battle of Hendtschoote obliged the Duke of York,
after some sharp out-post fighting, to abandon the siege, leaving from
forty to fifty pieces of heavy cannon, baggage, and military stores behind.

September 12th, 14th and 15th, the Coldstream marched through
Aven Capelle, Dixmuyde, and Rousselaer, towards Menin, when the
troops encamped,

Houchard was arrested by order of the French republican government, and sent to Paris. The charges preferred against him were—First,
that after defeating the English he did not drive them into the sea.
Secondly, that he sent no succours to the troops butchered at Cambray. Thirdly, that he abandoned Menin, and in his retreat exposed his
army to considerable danger. Houchard was found guilty on these
charges, and guillotined at Paris, November fifteenth, 1793.

There is no reason to suppose that Houchard was deficient in fidelity to his employers, or zeal for the cause in which he was embarked;
this commander seems to have been the victim of low cruelty and
ignorance. At that period the French armies were numerous, but badly
organised, and without generals of experience. Houchard's troops had
repeatedly been defeated; and when the loss of the Battle of Hendtschoote induced the British to relinquish the siege of Dunkirk, it
did not by any means follow that they were unable to make good
their retreat.

Napoleon, it is true, delighting to play the Jupiter-Scapin in public,
instructed his marshals to drive the English into the sea; and often told
his soldiers, that no such word as *impossible* existed in the French lan-

guage: but that accurate judge of military affairs never put his generals to death for not accomplishing what he knew to be impracticable.

The uninstructed and atrocious Jacobins in France, who had possessed themselves of the powers of government when Houchard was sent to the relief of Dunkirk, little qualified to distinguish between a retiring and a ruined army, conceived that because the Duke of York abandoned the siege, nothing remained for the French general but to destroy him. Whether the second and third charges against Houchard were better founded cannot now be ascertained with certainty; at the utmost, they rather afford evidence of incapacity than of treachery and cowardice.

Allowing them to be established, it must be admitted that the French commander was unfit for his situation, and that the interests of the cause he had undertaken to uphold required his dismissal: few persons however are forward in discovering their own deficiencies; and to a dispassionate mind the question naturally presents itself, how far those who employ a general of doubtful efficiency are less culpable than the individual they send forth at a venture to risk the lives of thousands in his probation. If the emigration had left the Jacobins no tried commanders at their disposal, the fact may perhaps be pleaded to excuse their making the hazardous selection, but will hardly justify the condemnation of Houchard to the guillotine for not being a man of intuitive genius.

On the seventeenth of September the following order was issued:—

> The Commander-in-Chief thanks the troops for the spirit with which they have gone through their late fatigues and distresses occasioned by long and rapid marches.

Quesnoy was taken by the Austrians, and the enemy defeated at Villiers en Couche. The Prince of Cobourg crossed the Sambre, and drove the French into their entrenchments at Maubeuge; while Marshal Clairfait threatened Cambray and Bouchain.

The Brigade of Guards marched through Menin and Courtray to Peck, (Oct. 10th), a village near Tournay, where they billeted two days; they then proceeded to St. Amand, and encamped between Quesnoy and Landrecy. The troops returned on the twenty-third by the same roads they had before passed.

About the end of October, (28th), the Third Guards with a detachment of the Fifteenth Light Dragoons attacked the enemy at Lannoy, and after two hours' fighting, succeeded in driving them from the village. From the twenty-ninth of this month to the eighth of November, the Coldstream was encamped on the plains of Gascogne; on the following day the campaign ended, and the Guards marched into barracks at Tournay. December 14th, the brigade of Guards moved to Ghent, where the Coldstream occupied St. Peter's barracks.

Return of Officers of the First battalion of the Coldstream on the Continent.

Comps.	Captains.	Lieutenants.	Ensigns.
Grenadier	Lieut.-Col. Wm. Morshead	Capt. Harry Calvert (Aid-de-camp to the Duke of York) ,, Richard Gregory ,, Charles Hotham, vice Calvert, appointed A.D.C.	
Colonel's Company.	H. R. H. the Duke of York's company	Capt. Lieut. Earl of Cavan	Richard Hulse Sir J. Shelly, vi Hulse promote
2d Major's Company	Col. Lowther Pennington	Capt. Wm. De Visme ,, John Calcraft, vice De Visme ,, J. Forbes, vice Calcraft	Wm. Lemon K. A. Howard Henry Bayly, vi Howard
	Lieut.-Col. George Fitz Roy	,, Charles Hotham ,, Roger Morris, vice Hotham	K. A. Howard Wm. Lemon, vi Howard
	Lieut.-Col. Tho. B. Bosville	,, John Calcraft ,, Hon. George Pomeroy, vice Calcraft	Hon. W. Fitz Ro
	Lieut.-Col. George Nugent	,, Wm. Wynyard	George H. Dyk
	Lieut-Col. T. E. Freemantle	,, Lord Say and Sele (to the Light Inf. Company)	Samuel Ongley
	Lieut.-Col. Hon. Edward Finch	,, Wm. Buller	Wm. Templeto Thomas Stibbe vice Templeto
	Lieut.-Col. Isaac Gascoyne	,, Hon. George Pomeroy ,, Wm. De Visme, vice Pomeroy	Richard Hulse Joseph Fuller, vi Hulse
Light Inf. company *	Lieut.-Col. George Eld	,, Lord Say and Sele ,, Charles Hotham	

Adjutant, Captain William Wynyard.
Quarter-Master, Samuel Lunt.
Surgeon's Mate, T. B. Hugo.
,, Edw. Alexis Giraud.

Camp at Menin, September 29th, 1793.

* The light infantry company, ordered to be raised by a King's warrant, dated April 19th 1793, and added to the establishment from 5th of June, embarked July 9th, 1793.

On the thirteenth His Royal Highness thanked the army for their conduct during the campaign.

The Duke of York quitted the army for London (Feb. 6th, 1794); Sir William Erskine was left in command during his absence.

19

CHAPTER 2

French defeated Near Cateau

On the first of March reinforcements embarked from England, amounting to eight hundred men for the brigade, of which two hundred were for the Coldstream.

A council of war assembled at Ath. It was proposed that Marshal Clairfait should take the command of all the auxiliary forces, and that the Duke of York should act under his orders.

★★★★★★

The following statement was published by the Convention early in 1794.*

REPUBLICAN ARMIES.		ARMIES OF THE COALESCED POWERS.	
Army of the North	. 222,000	Army of the Prince of Coburg . . .	. 140,000
United Armies of the Rhine and the Moselle	. . . 280,000	Army of the Duke of York . . .	. 40,000
Army of the Alps	. 60,000	Army appertaining to Holland . . .	. 20,000
Army of the Oriental Pyrenees	. . 80,000	Austrian Army on the Rhine . . .	. 60,000
Army of the South	. 60,000	Prussian Army .	. 64,000
Army of the West	. 80,000	Army of the Empire	. 20,000
Total 780,000		Army of Condé .	. 12,000
		Total 356,000	

* May be considered as exaggerated.

★★★★★★

After a month's delay, it was decided that the command should be given to the emperor, (April 9th), who arrived at Brussels,

A general movement was made throughout the army; the brigade of Guards marched by St. Leger to Vendegies sur l'Ecaillon, The emperor proceeded to Valenciennes, (April 16th), where, on the heights above Cateau, he reviewed the whole army, amounting to one hundred and eighty-seven thousand men, consisting of Austrians, British, Dutch, Hanoverians, and Hessians. At the conclusion of the review, the Guards pitched their tents for the first time this year.

✶✶✶✶✶✶

April 14.—The troops were furnished with straps for the purpose of carrying our greatcoats slung across the shoulders neatly rolled up. This in all sorts of weather was part of our equipment.— *Journal of Corporal Robert Brown of the Coldstream Guards.*

✶✶✶✶✶✶

On the following day, as the enemy were in force about Cambray, the army advanced in eight columns. The fourth and fifth were under the Duke of York. One of the columns under the immediate command of His Royal Highness was intended to carry the village of Vaux, Major-General Abercrombie commenced the attack, April 17th, supported by the grenadier companies of the First Guards under Colonel Stanhope, who stormed and gallantly took a battery.

At the same moment three battalions of Austrian grenadiers occupied the wood, and made themselves masters of the works which had been constructed. Nine cannon were taken during the day by the column under the Duke of York. Sir William Erskine was also successful with the troops under his orders, and gained possession of the redoubts and two pieces of cannon. The Coldstream lost four men killed, and one wounded. The village of Vaux having been plundered, was set on fire; the Duke of York was obliged to move to the battery that had been taken.

April 18th, the Coldstream and Third Guards marched through the wood of Leisse, but afterwards returned to Vaux. When relieved by General Abercrombie's corps, (19th), they continued their route through Cateau, and were posted on the Cambray road.

It being determined to lay siege to Landrecy, the direction of it was given to the Prince of Orange, whilst the emperor with his army protected the operations on the side of Guise, and the troops under the Duke of York covered Cambray. General Worms was stationed near Douay and Bouchain. Count Kaunitz defended the Sambre, and Clairfait held Flanders from Tournay to the sea.

On the twenty-third the Duke of York drove the enemy from Caesar's camp near Cambray. Some days after this, (26th),the heights of Cateau, which the British occupied, were attacked; but the enemy were repulsed with the loss of thirty-five pieces of cannon, and three hundred officers and men taken prisoners.

★★★★★★

The following order was issued by His Royal Highness the Duke of York, April 19th, 1794:

"An officer and forty men of the Guards to be immediately sent to Basuyaux, to enforce the order for preventing pillaging and burning houses, and the officer to inform General Otto of his arrival."

April 26th.—The enemy was repulsed in an attempt to raise the siege of Landrecy, and pursued by the cavalry to the gates of Cambray. On this occasion the Blues, 1st, 3rd, 5th Dragoon Guards, the Royals, 7th, 11th, and 16th Dragoons greatly distinguished themselves.

Extract from the General Order dated 12th of May, 1794.

All pieces of ordnance, colours, tumbrels, and horses taken from the enemy are to be delivered to the British artillery, and receipts taken for the same; application from the officer commanding the regiment who took them are, within three days, to be sent to Mr. Commissary Williamson, who, by order of His Royal Highness the Commander-in-Chief, will pay the following rewards, *viz.*—

For each cannon or howitzer	£20
For each pair of colours	£10
For each tumbrel	£10
For each horse	£12

★★★★★★

A large body of the enemy who attacked the Duke of York near Tournay, (May 3rd), was defeated. On this occasion General Harcourt, Major-General Dundas and Sir Robert Laurie distinguished themselves.

The emperor at length determined on making a general and simultaneous effort to drive the French out of the Low Countries. For this purpose, five columns of troops were ordered to advance; two of them were unable from fatigue to arrive in time; the others on reaching Moucron found the enemy too strong to be attacked, and retreated to Turcoin. (May 16th.)

★★★★★★

Here we find the solution of Buonaparte's Italian victories; his columns always arrived at the time indicated. Activity and combination could not fail to defeat superior forces under generals who seem to have planned simultaneous movements without knowing their ground, their distances, or what their troops could accomplish.

★★★★★★

The column led by the Duke of York, composed of seven English, five Austrian, and two Hessian battalions, with ten squadrons of cavalry, forced the enemy to evacuate Lannoy; the troops then halted. (His Royal Highness accompanied the centre column, consisting of the brigade of Guards, First Brigade of the line, and the free corps of O'Donnell.) They afterwards proceeded to Roubaix. General Abercrombie pushed on with the four battalions of Guards, and found the enemy strongly intrenched; they were cannonaded for some time. The flank battalion of Guards then advanced with the greatest regularity to storm, supported by the Seventh and Fifteenth Light Dragoons, who gallantly drove the French before them and took three guns

On the morning of the seventeenth the enemy attacked Turcoin; the same day a column from Lisle, and another corps, forced their way through General Otto's position at Waterloo, and assailed the rear of the British. When the advance parties from Lisle showed themselves between Roubaix and Mouveaux, it was impossible for the Duke of York to join the brigade of Guards. Abercrombie was directed to retreat by Roubaix, at which place the troops were to assemble, and the Coldstream had been posted to cover the communication. On reaching the heights of Roubaix, His Royal Highness was beset on all sides for three miles by repeated attacks of the enemy's artillery and cavalry; he therefore continued his retreat to Lannoy.

Finding that place in possession of the French, he went round the town under a heavy fire, and made his way through the fields to Templeuve. Major-General Fox was attacked by the Lisle column, and also retreated; but as his communication with the brigade of Guards and Lannoy was cut off, he joined General Otto. In this action Lieutenant-Colonel Gascoyne was wounded. The Coldstream lost one drummer, and fifteen rank and file killed, wounded, and missing.

During the conflict at Turcoin, the brigade of Guards and the heavy cavalry remained as a reserve in the camp at Templeuve, and

23

continued under arms all night. (The French have given a very exaggerated account of the action of Turcoin, and estimate the loss of the British at two thousand prisoners and sixty pieces of cannon.)

The position occupied by the British extended from the Scheld to the Orchies Road, and was secured by redoubts covering the front and flanks.

The Prince of Orange drove the enemy from Charleroi, before which town they had broken ground.

Such was the numerical superiority of the French, arising from their compulsatory system, that when one corps of troops was beaten, its place was immediately occupied by another.

At daybreak on the twenty-second of May, Pichegru with two hundred thousand men commenced a series of attacks on the position of the Allies: his troops advanced under a heavy fire of artillery; and after many unsuccessful efforts, having made no impression on the line, he was obliged, late in the evening, to retire. Major-General Fox and the Second Brigade made themselves conspicuous why the spirited manner in which they stormed and carried the village of Pontechin.

The sentiments of hostility entertained by the ruling party in the enemy's government against this country were so ferocious, as almost to exceed belief in the present day. The French Jacobins declared Mr. Pitt, the British Prime Minister, an enemy to the human race. They issued an order to their armies that no quarter should be given to the English or Hanoverians; an injunction scarcely to be paralleled in the darkest and most barbarous days of ancient warfare. This order was received with merited contempt by the brave men who composed the French armies; it was sent to the Republican troops with the following address:—

> England is capable of every outrage on humanity, and every crime towards the Republic. She attacks the rights of nations, and threatens to annihilate liberty. How long will you suffer the slaves of George to continue on your frontiers, the soldiers of the most atrocious of tyrants? He formed the Congress of Pilnitz, and brought about the disgraceful surrender of Toulon. He massacred our cities, and endeavoured to destroy the national representation. He starved your plains, and purchased treasons on the frontiers. When the events of battle should place in your power either English or Hanoverians, bring to remembrance the vast tracts of country English slaves have laid waste. Carry

your views to La Vendée, Toulon, Lyons, Landrecy, Martinico, and St, Domingo; places still reeking with blood, which the atrocious policy of the English has shed.

Do not trust to their artful language, which is an additional crime, worthy of their perfidious character and Machiavellian government. Those who boast that they abhor the tyranny of George, say, can they fight him? No! no! Republican soldiers: you ought, therefore, when victory shall put in your power either Englishmen or Hanoverians, to strike: not one of them ought to return to the traitorous territory of England, or to be brought into France. Let the British slaves perish, and Europe be free!

The Duke of York immediately noticed the sanguinary decree in terms worthy of his character and his country.

General Orders, June 7th.

His Royal Highness the Duke of York thinks it incumbent on him to announce to the British and Hanoverian troops under his command, that the National Convention of France, pursuing that gradation of crimes and horrors, which has distinguished the periods of its government as the most calamitous of any that has yet occurred in the history of the world, has just passed a decree that their soldiers shall give no quarter to the British or Hanoverian troops. His Royal Highness anticipates the indignation and horror which has naturally arisen in the minds of the brave troops whom he addresses, upon receiving this information.

His Royal Highness desires, however, to remind them, that mercy to the vanquished is the brightest gem in a soldier's character; and exhorts them not to suffer their resentment to lead them to any precipitate act of cruelty on their part, which may sully the reputation they have acquired in the world. His Royal Highness believes that it would be difficult for brave men to conceive that any set of men, who are themselves exempt from sharing in the dangers of war, should be so base and cowardly as to seek to aggravate the calamities of it upon the unfortunate people who are subject to their orders.

It was indeed reserved for the present times to produce to the world the proof of the possibility of the existence of such atrocity and infamy. The pretence for issuing this decree, even if founded in truth, would justify it only to minds similar to those of the members of the National Convention, it is in fact, too absurd to be noticed, and still less to be refuted. The French must themselves see through the flimsy artifice of an intended assassination, by which Robespierre has succeeded in procuring that military guard, which has at once established him the successor of the unfortunate Louis, by whatever name he may choose to dignify his future reign.

In all the wars which from the earliest times have existed between the English and the French nations, they have been accustomed to consider each other in the light of generous as well as brave enemies, while the Hanoverians, for a century the allies of the former, have shared in this reciprocal esteem. Humanity and kindness have at all times taken place the instant that opposition ceased; and the same cloak has been frequently seen covering those who were wounded, and enemies, whilst indiscriminately conveying to the hospitals of the conquerors.

The British and Hanoverian armies will not believe that the French nation, even under their present infatuation, can so far forget their characters as soldiers, as to pay any attention to a decree, as injurious to themselves as it is disgraceful to the persons who passed it; on this confidence His Royal Highness trusts that the soldiers of both nations will confine their sentiments of resentment and abhorrence to the National Convention alone; persuaded that they will be joined in them by every Frenchman who possesses one spark of honour, or one principle of a soldier: and His Royal Highness is confident that it will only be on findings contrary to every expectation, that the French Army has relinquished every title to the fair character of soldiers and of man, by submitting to, and obeying so atrocious an order, that the brave troops under his command will think themselves justified, and indeed under the necessity of adopting a species of warfare, for which they will stand acquitted to their own conscience, to their country, and the world: in such an event the French Army alone will be answerable for the tenfold vengeance which will fall upon themselves, their wives and their children, and their unfortunate country, already groaning under every calamity which the accumulated crimes of unprincipled ambition and avarice can heap upon their devoted victims.

His Royal Highness desires these orders may be read and explained to the men at their successive roll-callings.

To the credit of the French troops, neither officers nor soldiers carried the brutal commands of the Convention into execution; many of the superior officers positively refused to enforce the decree, and it was generally disregarded by their army.

The Princes of Cobourg and Orange, with General Beaulieu, attacked General Jourdan, who was strongly posted near Fleurus. This action continued till nearly the close of the day, when the Allied army was repulsed at all points. They took advantage of the night and retreated on Marbois and Nivelle, in the hope of reaching Namur.

The Duke of York, finding it impossible to form a Junction with Clairfait, retreated through Tournay to Romaux, (June 26th), where the troops under his command encamped till the third of July, when reinforcements arrived from England and landed at Ostend,

The four light infantry companies of the battalions of Guards at home embarked for the Continent on the fifth of July. The light infantry of the second battalion of the Coldstream consisted of Captain and Lieutenant-Colonel John Calcraft, Lieutenants and Captains John Stewart, and George Hart Dyke, five sergeants, five corporals, two buglers, and one hundred and fifty-four privates. (The establishment at this time was only ninety-five privates; the fifty-nine supernumeraries might have been to recruit the battalion.)

As the French occupied the country about Ostend, it was necessary for Lord Moira, who led the reinforcements, to make his way through all opposition and endeavour to join the Duke of York: this, by a rapid movement, he effected at Malines. July 9th.

Tournay, Ghent, and Ostend, all fell nearly at the same time into the hands of the French.

The light companies of the Guards, with a detachment for the Coldstream, arrived on the seventeenth: the light companies joined the flank battalion, now increased to twelve companies

July 23rd, the troops marched through West Wesel towards Rosendale; passed Breda, and encamped near Osterhout, (24th), at which place headquarters were established. On the first of September they moved to Berlicom. On the fourteenth the outposts were attacked along the Dourmel, and the troops of Hesse Darmstadt were forced with considerable loss.

The Duke of York at length thought it prudent to cross the Maese, and encamped at Wichen, (16th.)

The enemy were repulsed in their attempts to advance on the twenty-first and twenty-second of September.

Early in October the Duke of York concentrated his army about Nimeguen. On the twentieth a general attack was made on all the outposts. A few days after the enemy advanced towards Nimeguen. A change of position took place during the night of the thirtieth, when the Coldstream moved through Yoondon by Eelst, and arrived on the sixth of November at Sandyke.

The winter was unusually severe; before Christmas the Maese and Waal were frozen.

★★★★★★

A committee was formed at the Crown and Anchor in the Strand for supplying the army in Flanders with extra clothing; during the year the Coldstream was furnished with eight hundred and seven flannel waistcoats, and one hundred and fifty-nine pairs of shoes. A letter from His Royal Highness the Duke of York to William Devaynes, Esq. the Chairman, says, "His Royal Highness is fully sensible how much is due to the activity and spirit that have actuated the committee at which you preside, in forwarding what will tend so materially to preserve the health of the British soldiers in their present situation; and their grateful acknowledgements cannot be wanting to their country for the liberal provision it has made them."

★★★★★★

The enemy crossed the Maese, and another corps marched over the ice and took possession of the island of Bommel.

In January, 1795, Pichegru passed the Waal at several points, and made a general attack on the Allies, whose line extended between Nimeguen and Arnheim.

The Duke of York had previously returned to England, (on the sixth of December), in consequence of which the command devolved on General Walmoden, who had to contend with a victorious army greatly superior in number.

The brigade of Guards passed the Leck a second time on the tenth, and moved next day to the right of Rhenen.

The Allies were attacked and forced, and the Austrians abandoned Huessen, while the Hanoverians retired across the Lingen. At Rhenen the French were kept in check for a considerable time, and subsequently repulsed by the brilliant and spirited stand made by the brigade of Guards in conjunction with the infantry of the Prince of Salm. During the night the English retreated to Voorthuizen, taking with them their sick and wounded, with the exception of three hundred, who were left behind and treated by the French with great humanity.

The sufferings of the army during this retreat, in the severest part of one of the coldest winters known for some years in Holland, were of the most serious nature; the state of the sick and wounded was dreadful; many were frozen in the waggons and perished. The sixteenth of January was a day peculiarly memorable for the hardship and distress endured by the troops on their retreat to Deventer. The men had marched at the usual hour, and about three in the afternoon reached Welaw, where it was intended to halt for the night, but circumstances were such as to make it necessary to prolong the march fifteen miles further. The troops, besides suffering from the severity of the weather and from fatigue, had obtained no rations during the day.

The march was continued for about four miles over a sandy desert. The wind being excessively high, carried with it drifted snow and sand, with such violence that the human frame could hardly resist its power; the cold was intense; the water collected in the eyes of the men congealed as it fell, and hung in icicles from their eyelashes; the breath froze and lodged in incrustations of ice about the face, and on the blankets and coats wrapped round the soldiers. Numbers of men and women after dark lost sight of the column, and slept to wake no more. The troops reached Brickborge between ten and eleven at night, where the houses were already filled with Hessian soldiers, who opposed their admission in almost every instance; and it was only obtained at last by force or stealth.

★★★★★★

On the nineteenth of January the Prince of Orange embarked in an open boat at Scheveling: an immense crowd assembled at the Hague on the morning of his departure, and insisted on his being brought to trial for the part he had taken in favour of the English. His Guards however, protected him from all violence, and conducted him to the waterside, when he was again in danger till they dispersed the populace.

★★★★★★

Notwithstanding one of the most fatiguing and distressing marches ever experienced, the retreating army succeeded in conveying to Deventer all their ammunition, artillery, and military stores of every description. Fifty thousand French were eager in pursuit; and the English quitted Deventer, January 27th, only two days before it was entered by the enemy. Almost all the marches during this distressing retreat were made through roads covered with ice or snow, mud or water. The British crossed the Vecht, February 10th, and the River Ems. On the twenty-fourth of February they were overtaken by a portion of the French troops; but they displayed such courage and firmness that the efforts of the enemy to interrupt them were unavailing. The army therefore continued to retreat till it reached Bremen on the twenty-eighth of March, where it was joined by the two flank battalions. At this place headquarters and the brigade of Guards were stationed.

In taking a retrospective view of the campaign, the British troops will not be found deficient in their accustomed steadiness in the field, and habits of subordination and military discipline. From their manner of living, and the abundant supplies furnished by the commissariat department, they are seldom exposed to great privations. But when the want of food or clothing is experienced, as it in this campaign, or when the men, without sufficient shelter, are subject to hardships from the inclemency of the seasons, those evils are usually borne by them in a manner that evinces the superiority of the British soldier. The troops behaved, throughout the campaigns of 1793 and 1794, with a spirit that did them infinite credit, and especially during this arduous retreat.

★★★★★★

Soon after the commencement of the war with France it was resolved to detach a body of troops for the protection of Holland. Eighteen hundred Guards were accordingly embarked for that service in presence of the king and royal family at Greenwich.

They soon reached the place of destination, and their arrival, small as their numbers were, fortunately turned the tide of success against the French.

In, the course of two campaigns they distinguished themselves in Flanders on various occasions, particularly at Lincelles, where all the three battalions behaved to admiration.—*Grose's Military Antiquities* vol. 2.

★★★★★★

The Coldstream left Bremen on the eleventh of April, arrived at Willsdorf on the thirteenth, and embarked at Bremenlee next day on board the *Bellona* and *Loyal Briton* transports. After a tedious voyage, the first battalion was landed at Greenwich, (May 9th), and marched to their quarters in London. The men had eight days' leave granted them to see their friends.

CHAPTER 3

Expedition to Holland

An expedition to Ostend, May 1798, under General Coote, composed of about twelve hundred men, and the eight light companies of the First, Coldstream, and Third Guards, was fitted out for the purpose of destroying the basin, gates, and sluices of the Bruges canal, and intercepting the navigation between Ostend and Holland. (The four light companies of the First Guards did not disembark, having separated at sea.)

The command of the light infantry battalion devolved on Colonel Calcraft of the Coldstream, captain of the light company of the second battalion. Colonel the Honourable Edward Finch, who commanded the light company of the first battalion, having been accidentally wounded at a field-day on Barham Downs previous to the embarkation.

The transports sailed from Margate on the fourteenth of May, and as early as five o'clock on the morning of the nineteenth the troops, with artillery, miners, and every requisite, were on shore. About ten o'clock the sluice-gates and works were imperfectly blown up. ("His Majesty's Guards were conspicuous on all occasions on this service, and have added to their former laurels.")

The men were ordered to re-embark; but the surf and wind had so much increased; that to leave the shore became impracticable. General Coote, under these circumstances, thought fit to summon Ostend, (General Coote, in his dispatches, says "a feint"), to surrender, and received for answer "That the garrison must be first buried under the ruins." Coote then attempted to intrench himself on some sandhills near the coast.

Early on the morning of the twentieth he was attacked by several columns of the enemy; and after some ineffectual endeavours to contend against superior numbers, the troops surrendered as prisoners of war, when they were marched from Ostend through Lille into the citadel.

The officers belonging to the two companies of the Coldstream taken were Lieutenant-Colonel John Calcraft, Captains Thomas Armstrong and Willoughby Beane, and Assistant-Surgeon Fullelove.

★★★★★★

Loss of the Coldstream on the 20th of May: 4 rank and file killed, 2 drummers missing. Surrendered prisoners in the four companies of the Coldstream and Third, 2 captains and lieutenant-colonels, 5 lieutenants and captains, 1 quartermaster, 1 assistant-surgeon, 16 sergeants, 9 drummers, and 260 rank and file. Lieutenant-Colonel Campbell of the Third Guards not included, having died of his wounds.

★★★★★★

Several of the officers obtained leave to return to England the sooner to effect their exchange. (After being detained prisoners nine months the two companies were exchanged, and on their return landed at Dover, whence they marched to their quarters in London.)

This expedition may be added to the list of injudicious attempts made at various times by England on the Continent, without any object of importance, or national advantage, to be attained. Whatever damage was done to the sluices or canals between Bruges and Ostend could not be of material benefit to Great Britain, or of any great public injury to France.

This petty, vexatious, and buccaneering system of warfare has been much practised by the English, though it could only tend to keep up the flame of discord between hostile countries by adding the irritation of private injury to national conflict. It is to be hoped that civilisation is too far advanced, and the mutual interest of nations too well understood, to permit the recurrence of such acts of folly, inhumanity, and wasteful expenditure.

June 12th, the first battalions of the three regiments of Guards embarked at Portsmouth, and sailed for Ireland, where disturbances had broken out; the Coldstream were on board the *Queen Charlotte* and *Repulse*. Two battalions from the First and Third regiments of Guards were quartered at Waterford; the first battalion of the Coldstream, under Lieutenant-Colonel Gascoyne, at Ross. The brigade was under the command of Major-General Stanwix.

Officers.	Officers absent.	Non-Com. Officers.	Rank & File.	Sick.	Total.	Wanting to complete.	Total establishment.
62	25	135	1747	130	2099	523	2622

OFFICERS OF THE COLDSTREAM GUARDS IN IRELAND FROM JUNE, 1798.

Major-Gen. Slaughter Stanwix.	Ensign Montagu Wynyard.
Colonel Andrew Cowell.	,, George Morgan.
,, Hon. Edward Finch.	,, Gilbert Stirling.
,, Isaac Gascoyne.	,, Charles Phillips.
Lt.-Col. C. Howard Bulkely.	,, Charles Vis'. Petersham.
,, Arthur Brice.	,, Lord Charles Bentinck.
,, Edm. Lord Dungarvon.	,, George Sidley.
Lt. & Capt. K. A. Howard.	,, John Thompson.
,, ,, H. Bayly.	,, Hon. A. Duncan.
,, ,, Hilton Jolliffe.	,, Matthew Onslow.
,, ,, Hon. C. G. M'Lellan.	,, John Frederick.
,, ,, Tho. Stubbert.	Quarter-Master John Holmes.
,, ,, Jas. Phillips.	Surgeon George Rose.
,, ,, Rich. Boulton.	Assistant do. John Simpson.
,, ,, J. Allen Lloyd.	,, ,, John Gilham.
,, ,, K. D. Jackson.	

At this time the grenadier battalion, composed of eight companies, four from the Firsts two from the Coldstream, and the same number from the Third Guards, with the third battalion of the First Guards, formed the First Brigade of Guards under Major-General D'Oyley. The first battalion of the Coldstream and that of the Third Guards under Major-General Burrard formed the Second Brigade.

In July, 1799, by the military arrangements entered into between the Confederate Courts and Great Britain, it was agreed that a diversion should be attempted by sending an expedition to invade Holland, in conjunction with twenty thousand auxiliaries to be furnished by Russia. Early in August twelve thousand men assembled on the coast of Kent, and an equal number were preparing to meet at the same point.

The brigade of Guards under MajorGeneral Burrard left the camp at Barham Downs for Sandwich, on August 7th. They embarked at Ramsgate on the twelfth, and sailed with the first division under Sir Ralph Abercrombie. Contrary winds prevented the English fleet, commanded by Lord Duncan, from reaching the Texel till the twenty-seventh. The disembarkation, which was covered by Vice-Admiral

Mitchell, took place near the Helder Point. The troops had scarcely begun to move forward when the right was briskly attacked by a considerable Dutch force under General Daendels: the attack was repeated with fresh troops, but the enemy were repulsed after a severe contest, and retired to a position two leagues further in the rear.

Towards the close of the day Major-General D'Oyley's brigade of Guards was brought into action, and suffered some loss. The Coldstream lost seven rank and file wounded, one missing. The casualties among the men of the two grenadier companies are necessarily omitted during the campaign, as they were not separately stated from that of the battalion of grenadiers. Late at night the garrison of a fort at the Helder Pointy consisting of nearly two thousand national troops, withdrew. Next morning the works were occupied by the British.

The passage of the Texel being opened, the Dutch fleet lying near the Vlieter surrendered to Admiral Mitchell. In the meantime, September 1st, till the expected reinforcements should arrive from England, Sir Ralph Abercrombie entrenched his troops in the peninsula of the Helder. The British were in position along the Groot Sluys of the Zype, with Oude Sluys on Zuider Zee on the left, and Petten on the North Sea on their right. Abercrombie, apprised of the enemy's intention, took the necessary precautions.

At daybreak on September 10th, the French and Batavians attacked the entrenchments in three columns, on the right and centre. One of the enemy's columns, composed of Dutch, commanded by General Daendels, moved on the village of St. Martin; a second under General de Monceau, also composed of Dutch, moved on Crabbendam and Zyper Sluys; the French left assailed that part of the position occupied by the brigade of Guards under Major-General Burrard. They were received with determined courage, and everywhere driven back. About ten o'clock the enemy retreated towards Alkmaar, leaving many killed and wounded, one gun and a number of waggons and pontoons.

Sir Ralph Abercrombie in his dispatch says:

> It is impossible for me to do full justice to the conduct of the troops. The two brigades of Guards repulsed with great vigour the column of French which had advanced to attack them, and where the slaughter of the enemy was great. (Sir Ralph Abercrombie's dispatch—*London Gazette Extraordinary*, Sept. 16, 1799. No. 15182.)

This affair cost the enemy one thousand killed and wounded, and the Allies about two hundred.

The loss of the Coldstream was one rank and file killed, eight wounded. After the action the army re-occupied its position.

The Duke of York landed in Holland, September 13th, and took the command of the army. Soon after the Russian contingent and all the forces destined for the expedition arrived, when it was determined to commence offensive operations.

Two hours before daybreak on the nineteenth all were in readiness to attack the lines of General Brune in front of Alkmaar. The right column consisted of twelve Russian battalions, the Seventh Light Dragoons, and General Manners's brigade under the Russian General d'Herman, extending to the sand-hills on the coast near Camperdown, where part of the enemy had posted themselves most advantageously. The next column was commanded by Lieutenant-General Dundas, and consisted of two squadrons of the Eleventh Light Dragoons, the two brigades of Guards, and Prince William of Gloucester's brigade. Two squadrons of the Eleventh Light Dragoons and the brigades of Major-Generals Don and Coote formed the third column, under Sir James Pulteney.

The left column, under Lieutenant-General Sir Ralph Abercrombie, was composed of two squadrons of the Eighteenth Dragoons, and the brigades of the Earl of Chatham, Major-General Moore, and the Earl of Cavan; besides four battalions, one of grenadiers, and one of light infantry of the line, and the Twenty-Third and Fifty-Fifth regiments under Colonel MacDonald. The intention was to outflank both wings of the enemy. Sir Ralph Abercrombie was detached to Hoorn in rear of the Dutch, who formed the enemy's right. The First Brigade of Guards moved from Tatenhoorn and Krabendaw, on the left of the Alkmaar canal, to co-operate with the corps under Major-General Sedmorabzen in attacking Schoreldam. The Second Brigade of Guards, under Major-General Burrard, was to keep up the communication with the column under Sir James Pulteney.

General Herman attacked the front and left of the enemy's line, which gave way; the Russian column, however, was placed in a critical position. From having advanced too far, they were nearly surrounded, and the village of Bergen, which had been for some time in their occupation, was retaken by General Vandamme at the point of the bayonet. The Russians had given themselves up to plunder, and being unsupported, were, after a gallant contest, almost destroyed. Had they shown on this occasion as much discipline as intrepidity, they might have retained the ground they had gained. General Herman was made prisoner, and General Esseu dangerously wounded,

The right wing of the Batavian Army under General Daendels was opposed to the British, who maintained their position till past twelve p.m., when they retired in consequence of the defeat of the Russian column. The Duke of York endeavoured to repair the disorder occasioned by their misconduct, and immediately attacked the village of Schorel with General Manners's brigade, supported by three Russian battalions, the brigade of Guards, and the Thirty-Fifth regiment, commanded by Prince William. As all attempts to retrieve the disaster at Bergen proved ineffectual, after carrying Schorel, the commander-in-chief withdrew his left. Sir Ralph Abercrombie also quitted the post of Hoorn during the night, and the two armies resumed their former positions.

The British in this encounter lost one hundred and twenty killed, four hundred wounded, and five hundred missing. The French stated their loss to be one hundred and fifty killed, and three hundred wounded. That of the Russians was considerable.

The casualties in the Coldstream were, Lieutenant-Colonel Morris of the grenadier battalion of Guards killed, one sergeant, nine rank and file killed; Lieutenant-Colonel Cunynghame, one sergeant, and twenty-one rank and file wounded; one sergeant and thirteen rank and file missing, Reinforcements of upwards of four thousand Russians landed at the Helder on the twenty-sixth, and marched to join their main body.

The inclemency of the weather compelled the contending armies to remain opposite each other till the second of October, when the Duke of York attacked the enemy's lines. "The points where this well-fought battle was principally contested, were from the sea-shore in front of Egmont, extending along the sandy desert, or height, above Bergen", (the Duke of York's dispatch—*London Gazette Extraordinary*, Oct. 18, 1799. No. 15190): the contest was severe, and continued from six o'clock a.m. till the same hour in the evening. Sir Ralph Abercrombie commanded the right, Lieutenant-General Dundas the centre, and Major-General Burrard the left. After a gallant resistance the enemy were totally defeated, and retired in the night from their ground on the Lange Dyke, the Koe Dyke at Bergen, and from their extensive range of sand-hills between the latter place and Egmont-op-Zee to a still stronger position at Beverwick, three leagues from Haarlem.

The victory was attended with a loss of more than two thousand men; that of the enemy exceeded four thousand killed, three hundred prisoners, seven pieces of cannon, and many tumbrels.

The British took possession of Alkmaar on October 3rd; and on the sixth, the Duke of York, knowing the enemy expected reinforcements, thought it expedient again to attack, and, if possible, to force them to retire "before they had an opportunity of strengthening by works the short and very defensible line which they occupied." The British and Russians first gained possession of the villages of Limmen and Baccum. The enemy advanced, and the action became general along the whole line from Limmen to the sea, and continued with great obstinacy on both sides till dark, when they retreated, leaving the Confederates masters of the field.

The following is an extract from His Royal Highness the Duke of York's dispatch, dated "Headquarters, Alkmaar, October 7th, 1799";—

Nor ought I to omit the praise due to Colonel Clephane, commanding four companies of the Third, and one company of the Coldstream regiment of Guards, who by a spirited charge drove two battalions of the enemy from the post of Archer Sloot, making two hundred prisoners.

The loss of the Allies was two thousand five hundred and fifty-five killed, wounded, and prisoners. The Coldstream lost one man killed, thirteen wounded, and three rank and file missing.

The Duke of York ascertained that since the second, the enemy had been reinforced by six thousand infantry, and their position at Beverwick considerably improved. These were obstacles which it would be necessary to remove previous to making any attempt on Haarlem. The enemy had also detached a strong force to Purmirind, which, if the Duke of York's army advanced, would be left in his rear. His Royal Highness, therefore, taking these circumstances into consideration, together with the want of supplies of every description and the impracticable state of the roads, judged it advisable to withdraw from his advanced position, and wait for further instructions from England,

Subsequently the Allies concentrated in their entrenchments within the Helder Point. Alkmaar and Hoorn were again occupied by the enemy, who nearly surrounded the Allied camp. In face of the French Army it would have been dangerous to attempt to re-embark: on the other hand, the English had it in their power to cut the dykes, which would devastate the country. A convention was therefore signed on the eighteenth of October, which provided that the British and Russian Army should embark as soon as possible without committing any injury, and that eight thousand French and Dutch prisoners of war, then detained in England, should be restored unconditionally to their respective countries.

The army commenced their re-embarkation on the twenty-second. The first battalion of the Coldstream landed at Yarmouth on the thirty-first, and marched to their quarters in Upper Westminster. The grenadier battalion, in which were the grenadier companies of the Coldstream, disembarked at Ramsgate.

OFFICERS OF THE COLDSTREAM GUARDS IN HOLLAND, 1799.

Colonel Hon. Edward Finch.		Captain James Phillips.	
Lt.-Col. C. Howard Bulkely.		,,	Richard Boulton.
,,	Hon. James Forbes.	,,	John Allen Lloyd.
,,	Roger Morris.	,,	Rich. Downes Jackson.
,,	Arthur Brice.	Ensign Sir John Gordon, Bart.	
,,	Edmund Earl of Cork.	,,	George Morgan.
,,	John Leveson Gower.	,,	Gilbert Sterling.
,,	Francis Cunynghame.	,,	Charles Phillips.
,,	K. A. Howard.	,,	Richard Beadon.
Capt.-Lieut. Thos. Armstrong.		,,	John Thompson.
Captain Henry Bayly.		,,	John Frederick.
,,	Henry Mac Kinnon.	,,	W. T. Myers.
,,	M. Warren Peacocke.	,,	L. F. Adams.
,,	Hilton Jolliffe.	Quarter-Master John Holmes.	
,,	Hon. C. Grey M'Lellan.	Surgeon George Rose.	
,,	Thomas Stibbert.	Assistant do. John T. Simpson.	
,,	Hon. John Wingfield.	,,	John Gilham.
,,	William Sheridan.		

CHAPTER 5.

War with France

In May, 1798, General Buonaparte had sailed from Toulon for Egypt with a large force, and the French continued to hold possession of that country.

On the eighteenth of August, 1800, eight companies of the first battalion of the Coldstream embarked at the Cove of Cork on board two sixty-four gunships, the *Dictator* and *Delft*, and joined an expedition under Sir James Pulteney, against Vigo, which produced no result. They then proceeded from Vigo to the Mediterranean, where they united with the army under Sir Ralph Abercrombie, which after some delay reached Marmorice Bay.

The second division also arrived in a few days. The cavalry and sick were put on shore, and the regiments landed in succession.

The expedition remained some time on the coast of Asia Minor, and sailed on the twenty-second of February from Marmorice with the daring purpose of wresting Egypt from the grasp of that celebrated army of Italy, whose achievements in Europe had filled the civilized world with admiration and astonishment.

The veteran comrades of Buonaparte, notwithstanding the losses they had sustained in their contests with the Turks and Mamelukes, were still greatly superior in numbers to the troops, (see list following), under Abercrombie; they were besides in possession of the resources of the country and of all its strongholds, which had been fortified with the utmost skill and care. Eighteen months' occupation had inured the French to the burning suns of Egypt, which had become their adopted country, and they confidently prepared to repel the meditated attack.

Including 1000 sick, and 500 Maltese.

Guards.	Major-Gen. Hon. George J. Ludlow

RESERVE.

1st or Roy^b	
Two bat^m of	Major-Gen.
the 54th	Coote
92d	

8th	
13th	
19th	Maj.-Gen. Cradock
90th	

2d	
50th	Major-Gen. Lord
79th	Cavan

18th	
30th	Brigadier-General
44th	John Doyle
89th	

Minorca	
De Rolle's	Major-General John
Dillon's	Stuart

Reserve (right column, under Maj.-Gen. Moore):

- 40th Flank companies
- 23d
- 28th
- 42d
- 58th
- Corsican Rangers
- Detachment 11th Dragoons
- Do. Hompesch's Dragoons

12th Dragoons	Brigadier-Gen.
26th Do.	Finch

Artillery and	Brigadier-Gen.
Pioneers	Lawson

The British were strangers to that ungenial climate, and laboured under all the debilitating consequences of a protracted voyage and long confinement on shipboard: but without pausing to calculate disadvantages, they cheerfully proceeded to accomplish their country's errand.

March 1st, 1801, the day previous to anchoring in Aboukir Bay it was given out that the brigade of Guards was to be in the first line.

The following order was issued on the fourth of March:—

The troops will hold themselves in readiness to land as soon as the weather permits. The first division that disembarks, consisting of the brigade of Guards, reserve, 2nd battalions of the Royals, and 54th regiments, will carry their blankets and three days' provisions, and will leave their knapsacks on board.

The weather was unfavourable; but becoming more moderate at two o'clock on the morning of the eighth, the first division, consisting of the reserve under Major-General Moore, the brigade of Guards under Major-General the Honourable James Ludlow, the Royals, the first battalion of the Fifty-Fourth regiment, and part of the second battalion, with some other detachments, the whole being under the command of Major-General Coote, got into the boats and pushed off for their rendezvous, some hundred paces from the shore. Each flank was protected by light armed vessels, and several bombs and gun-brigs were moored with their broadsides to the beach.

At nine o'clock the signal was given. About two thousand French were advantageously posted on the top of some sand-hills; the centre of their position was nearly two hundred feet above the level of the sea, on which were planted twelve pieces of cannon. These guns, as well as the castle of Aboukir, commanded the landing. When the boats approached, they were assailed with grape and musketry from the shore. The reserve jumped out of their boats, formed, and pushed forward: the Twenty-Third and Fortieth regiments gallantly charged the height, and kept advancing to the two hills in the rear. The Forty-Second regiment gained the summit, notwithstanding a heavy discharge of grape-shot, and the opposition of a considerable force of infantry: on reaching the top, they were charged by a body of dragoons, who were however repulsed.

On landing, the Guards were suddenly attacked by the same dragoons, who had rallied. The Fifty-Eighth regiment, which had already formed on the rights opened a fire, under cover of which the Guards were enabled to show front, when the enemy's cavalry suffered greatly. The Fifty-Fourth regiment and Royals reached the shore at the moment when a hostile column was advancing against the left of the Guards: on perceiving them, the French gave one discharge and retired. The heights were then occupied by the British, and, General Coote with the Guards coming up, the French retired behind the sand-hills.

The loss of the enemy amounted to nearly four hundred; that of the British to seven hundred and forty-two men. In the Coldstream the casualties were, Ensign Warren and seventeen rank and file killed; Captains Plunkett, Frederick, Beadon, and Myers, Surgeon Rose, eleven sergeants, one drummer, and fifty-seven rank and file wounded. Captain Frederick and Surgeon Rose died or their wounds.

Aboukir Castle still held out, (surrendered on the thirteenth): it was blockaded by the Queen's regiment and the Twenty-Sixth dismounted Dragoons.

March 9th, 1801, the British troops were ordered to make a movement in advance: the next day they approached the enemy, when some skirmishing took place. On the eleventh the following General Order was issued:—

> The army will advance tomorrow; the brigade of Guards marching from the right will lead the first column: they will proceed along the road near the sea-beach, facing the redoubts of Mandora to the left.

Sir Ralph Abercrombie next day (12th), moved to Mandora Tower, where the army encamped. The light troops of the enemy engaged the piquets nearly the whole march, which did not exceed four miles. The French, having received reinforcements from Cairo and Rosetta, had increased their strength to about thirty guns and six thousand men, including cavalry.

On the thirteenth the enemy occupied a strong position on a rising ground, the ascent to which was gradual; their right extended towards the canal of Alexandria, their left to the sea, Abercrombie, whose troops were in two lines, formed them into columns of battalions, left in front, with the intention of attacking the enemy's right. When the British advanced, the French moved down from their position, and directed a spirited fire of musketry and artillery on the Ninety-Second regiments. The enemy's cavalry at the same time charged the extreme right, and came in contact with the Ninetieth regiment, commanded by Colonel Graham, since created Lord Lynedoch. This corps with undaunted courage awaited their approach, and at the exact moment threw in a volley, which obliged the French cavalry to swerve to the right previous to their flight.

The English formed in two lines, the reserve in column on the right. The Guards supported the centre. General John Stuart's and Doyle's brigades moved in column to rear of the left. All preserving the greatest order steadily advanced under a heavy fire of artillery and musketry. The French were forced to retire through a plain of three miles to their lines in front of Alexandria.

The English lost twelve hundred and eighty-four killed and wounded; the French about five hundred, with four guns. Ensign Jenkinson of the Coldstream was killed, and Captain Beadon wounded; two rank and file killed, and four wounded, Major-General Cradock distinguished himself; it was principally owing to his excellent arrangements that the enemy's cavalry was repulsed. The French colonel, Latour Maubourg, was dangerously wounded.

Lieutenant-Colonel Brice of the Coldstream Guards commanded the piquets on the fourteenth, when he was attracted by some firing, and, proceeding to the spot, was wounded and taken prisoner, and died two days after. (Sir Robert Wilson, in his *Expedition to Egypt*, says, "he missed his way when going his rounds, which it was almost impossible to prevent." Walsh, in his *Campaign*, also gives the same account.)

The British troops in every encounter from the time of their landing had shown themselves decidedly superior to the French. Their position was about four miles from Alexandria, with the sea on their right flank, and the Lake of Aboukir on the left. In front of the centre a considerable plain extended as far as the elevated ground on which the enemy had entrenched themselves. The Twenty-Eighth and Fifty-Eighth regiments were posted among some ancient ruins and redoubts on the rights supported by the Twenty-Third, Fortieth, Forty-Second, and the Corsican Rangers. Between the right and the light centre, occupied by the Guards on a rising ground, was a flat, on which there were some cavalry.

From the hill where the Guards stood the line ran obliquely to the left, at the end of which two batteries were intended to be constructed, and were in a state of forwardness. On the left of the Guards the Ninety-Second, Second, Fifty-Fourth, First, Eighth, Eighteenth, Ninetieth, and Thirteenth regiments were stationed in *échelon*, ready if necessary, to form on the Guards. The second line was composed of the regiments of Minorca, De Rollers, Dillon's, the Queen's, Forty-Fourth, Eighty-Ninth, Twelfth, and the Twenty-Sixth Dragoons.

The troops under the French General Menou, recently arrived from Grand Cairo, occupied a strong defensive position on some steep hills. In front of their right ran a strip of land joining the canal, which occasioned the left of the English to stand in the oblique position before described. (The city and Pharos of Alexandria, with Pompey's Pillar and Cleopatra's Needle, were distinctly to be seen from the English camp).

An hour before day on the morning of the twenty-first of March, General Menou, with his army increased to thirteen thousand men, and about equal to the English, made a false attack on the left; but the report of musketry soon announced that the right was the point he really intended to assault. The British awaited the enemy's approach with great composure: the latter advanced with loud huzzas and drums beating; Colonels Paget and Houstoun, however, whose regiments held the key of the position, would not permit a shot to be fired till they were close at hand, when the troops were ordered to open their fire, which obliged the French to retreat. The enemy then wheeled to their right for the purpose of surrounding a redoubt; a second column attacked in front, and a third penetrated the ruins before mentioned.

At this moment Colonel Crowdjye with the Fifty-Eighth, after two or three rounds, rushed on them with the bayonet; this charge was supported by the Twenty-Third. The Forty-Second seized the opportunity, and advanced in the most gallant manner to cover the open space at which the column had entered, who after great loss surrendered. The Twenty-Eighth, the Forty-Second, and Fifty-Eighth regiments, and the flank companies of the Twenty-Third and Forti-eth under Colonel Spencer, greatly distinguished themselves. General Stuart came up with his brigade, which quickly threw the enemy into disorder, and at length forced them to a precipitate flight. It was at this critical moment that Sir Ralph Abercrombie received his mortal wound. (Sir Ralph Abercrombie died on board the *Foudroyant* on the 28th of March.)

At daybreak a strong column of French grenadiers, supported by a line of infantry, attacked the position occupied by the Guards, whose skirmishers were driven in. The enemy s intention was to turn the left flank of the brigade, all the troops being placed in *échelon*. On the near approach of the French, several companies of the left battalion were thrown back. By a steady and incessant fire, together with the advance of General Coote's brigade, they completed the confusion of the enemy, who had already shown an inclination to waver. The attack was principally confined to the right and centre. General Menou, finding all his attempts unsuccessful, retreated, after a last effort to carry the position by a charge of cavalry under Brigadier-General Roize, sup-ported by General Regnier with the divisions under Lanusse, Ram-pon, and Friant. (General Roize was killed with many distinguished officers, and the French cavalry completely broken and almost de-stroyed.—*General Regnier's State of Egypt.*)

The loss of the English was fourteen hundred and sixty-four men. Between three and four thousand French were left on the field of bat-tle. The casualties in the Coldstream Guards were, seven rank and file killed, one sergeant, fifty-two rank and file wounded.

The following general orders were given out by Lord Hutchinson:

Major-General Ludlow and the brigade of Guards will accept the thanks of His Excellency the Commander-in-Chief for the cool, steady, and soldier-like manner in which they repulsed the attack of the enemy's column.

The Coldstream remained in camp before Alexandria. On the eighth of July a reinforcement for the regiment of one hundred and fifty men arrived in the *Active* frigate; they were conveyed across the lake in boats belonging to the fleet, and landed at the depot. On the ninth of August Major-General the Earl of Cavan was appointed to take command of the brigade of Guards.

★★★★★★

State of the first battalion Coldstream Guards in camp, four miles from Alexandria, March 30th. Two captains, eleven lieutenants, four ensigns, thirty-two sergeants, twelve drummers, six hundred and forty-seven rank and file, two hundred and three sick.

★★★★★★

On the sixteenth of August, a corps under General Coote, including the Guards, was embarked on the Lake Mareotis, and sent to the westward. Three battalions of Brigadier-General Finch's brigade had been previously despatched in a number of barks, (Walsh's *Egypt*, vol 2, about 400); these had drifted to leeward during the night, and considerably retarded the landing. When the troops were on shore, a position was taken along a ridge of quarries about half a mile broad, at the foot of which was a sandy plain that extended to the sea; the breadth of this peninsula did not exceed two miles. There was a small island opposite the western division, on which stood Fort Marabout. On the evening of the eighteenth, General Coote advanced about two miles and occupied position, the Guards extending across the quarries; the rest of the troops formed *en potence*, facing the sea.

At six o'clock p.m., (21st) after the guns of Marabout had been dismounted by the batteries, the garrison capitulated. The Coldstream had two rank and file wounded.

General Coote marched at daylight in three columns. The Coldstream and Third Guards under Lord Cavan formed two columns on the right, and General Ludlow's brigade the third. Major-General Finch's brigade was in reserve: the advanced guard, consisting of the Twenty-Seventh, with some of Lowenstein's riflemen, and two hundred of the Guards, were under Lieutenant-Colonel Jolliffe of the Coldstream. Next morning, at four o' clocks the British piquets fell in with and drove in the French outposts. The columns entered the plain at daylight, and kept gallantly moving on under a sharp cannonade.

★★★★★★

"The Guards on the right had continued their march indifferent to the grape which played upon them, forcing, by their steady progress, the French to evacuate the battery opposed to them."—Sir Robert Wilson's *Egypt*, vol. 2.

Sir Robert Wilson also mentions a singular escape of General Coote and a company of Guards, who were passing under a heavy fire of grape, which struck off several of the men's caps without doing any injury.

★★★★★★

The Turks took possession of Sugar-loaf Hill on the right. The Coldstream had two wounded.

On the twenty-fourth General Spencer landed with Brigadier-General Blake's brigade, and some Mamelukes also joined General Coote's division, besides about seven hundred Turks. Several ships of war entered the harbour for the purpose of protecting the left of the line. Next day a battery opened from eight heavy guns and mortars against the *redoute des Bains*.

After dark Lieutenant-Colonel Smith with the Twenty-Sixth regiment and some dragoons, supported by Lieutenant-Colonel Layard, attacked and drove in the left of the enemy's piquets in the most spirited manner with the bayonet, the men not having even loaded their muskets. The batteries continued firing on the eastern side of the town till twelve, when the enemy's fire ceased; it was soon discovered that they had withdrawn their guns, in the evening an *aide-de-camp* of General Menou presented a letter at the advanced posts, proposing a suspension of hostilities for three days, with a view to settle terms.

An answer in the affirmative was returned, and all hostilities were to cease, on the French firing three guns loaded with blank cartridge, to be answered in the same manner by the English, when the standards of both armies were to be lowered. On the evening of the twenty-ninth, Menou sent by his *aide-de-camp* to request a prolongation of the truce for thirty-six hours, which was rejected. The French general begged to be allowed till two o'clock the following day. The capitulation was concluded without further delay by Brigadier-General Hope, who was received by the French general with great politeness, and invited to dine; the dinner consisted entirely of horse-flesh.

The garrison of Alexandria, which surrendered on the first of September, amounted to nearly twelve thousand, including five thousand nine hundred and sixty-five soldiers of artillery, cavalry, and infantry, besides marine artillery, sappers, miners, and seamen doing garrison-duty, &c. &c.

The other division of the French Army having surrendered at Cairo, the enemy were no longer in possession of any part of Egypt; and the object of the expedition being attained, Lord Cavan delivered to the Captain Pacha the keys of the city of Alexandria. The army shortly after prepared for embarkation. (September 26th.)

Blame has been attached by some French writers to General Menou, for not opposing the invaders with his whole force. It may also have accorded with the selfish policy of Buonaparte, that the odium of an unsatisfactory termination to an enterprise planned by himself, should be ascribed to mismanagement after his departure. But threatened by the approach of the Indian Army under Sir David Baird, and embarrassed by the questionable fidelity of the Egyptian population, Menou doubtless felt the necessity of leaving a considerable force at Cairo.

Well aware that the British on their debarkation must enter the field subject to many disadvantages, he met them with an army equal in numbers, and superior in artillery and cavalry. Such comparative means Buonaparte himself would have deemed sufficient to face and overthrow the veterans of Austria in his Italian campaigns; nor, had he been in Egypt at the period of the Battle of Alexandria, would he have allowed it to be said, that to enable his boasted invincibles to attack the islanders with success, it was necessary to bring against them an overwhelming superiority of twice their numbers, Menou at that period, like his great master in the art of war, had no conception of the qualities of British troops; but he knew that he had under his command the celebrated army of Italy, which had victoriously contended against the finest armies of the European Continent.

With this experience of Austrian warfare, and with a well-founded confidence in his men, Menou challenged his antagonists to a combat on nearly equal terms, and was, to his great surprise, defeated. He found, when too late, that he had miscalculated the prowess of the British soldiery. A few years after, the same rough lesson was taught Napoleon.

The first battalion of the Coldstream arrived at Malta on the seventeenth of October, landed the next day, and went into barracks, where they remained three weeks, Afterwards they re-embarked, landed in separate divisions between the sixth and twenty-ninth of December at Portsmouth, and marched from Winchester on Friday the eighth of January, 1802. In a few days they reached London.

Return of the Officers of the first battalion of the Coldstream in the expedition to Egypt :—

	Captains.	Lieutenants.	Ensigns.
Grenr. Compy.	At home		
	H. R. H. the Duke of York's company	Capt. Lt. H. F. Bouverie Capt. F. Adam	G. T. B. Warren
1st Maj.	Maj.-Gen. Earl of Cavan	,, Hon. Ed. Plunkett ,, T. L. Campbell	John Hamilton
	Col. Hon. Edward Finch	,, John Thompson ,, James Philps	George Collier
	,, Brice	,, Sir I. Gordon	Richard Beckett
	,, Earl of Cork	,, Sir Gilbert Stirling ,, Chs. Philips	Thos. Roberts
	Lt.-Col. H. MacKinnon	,, Richd. Beadon ,, John Frederick	T. W. Brotherton
	,, ,, Hilton Jolliffe	,, Thos. Stibbert ,, Chs. Fane	Lord Delvin
	,, ,, W. M. Peacock	,, Edd. Dalling ,, W. Myers	Jenkinson
Light Compy.	At home		

Adjutant, Sir Gilbert Stirling.
Quarter-Master, John Holmes.
Surgeon, George Rose.
Assistant Surgeon, John Gilham.
       ,,   ,,   H. Fearon.
Drum-Major, William Lamb.
Deputy-Marshall, William Alpe.

Changes that took place.

Ensigns Warren and Jenkinson killed; Col. Brice, Capt. Frederick, and Surgeon Rose, died of their wounds.

Joined.	Returned to England.
Capt. Geo. Sedley	Capt. Hon. Edd. Plunkett
Ensign, Hon. Edd. Acheson	,, Sir Gilbert Stirling
Lieut.-Col. G. H. Dyke	,, ,, ,, Sedley
	,, H. F. Bouverie
	Surgeon, John Gilham
	Lt.-Col. H. MacKinnon, via Germany, &c.

The treaty of Amiens put an end to hostilities, March 25th, 1802. During this peace Buonaparte was made President of the Cisalpine Republic. Louisiana, the Duchy of Parma, and the Island of Elba, were ceded to France by the private treaty with Spain. An amnesty was granted to all emigrants who had not borne arms against the revolutionists; Buonaparte had been declared First Consul for life, and was empowered to appoint his successor. The Legion of Honour was instituted by him for the encouragement of military, naval, and scientific men, and also of those most eminent in the administration of affairs.

On the twelfth of May the English Ambassador quitted France, and hostilities between England and the French Government recommenced. May 18th, the First Consul threatened, to invade England, which created considerable alarm, and the nation was placed in a state of defence.

The British Government seized all the French ships they could find, making the crews prisoners. Sixty thousand seamen were voted by Parliament, and the army was increased to one hundred and twenty-nine thousand men. An army of Reserve was raised, and volunteer corps were formed throughout the country.

The first battalion marched to Chelmsford, June 27th, 1803, when they were brigaded with the first battalion of the Third Guards, under the command of Major-General the Honourable Edward Finch, On the tenth of August the brigade was inspected by His Royal Highness the Duke of York, in the main street at Chelmsford. It was from this place that the subjoined letter, so highly creditable to the brigade, was addressed to the Secretary of the Patriotic Fund:—

Chelmsford New Barracks, August 19, 1803.

Gentlemen,

Impressed with a due sense of the cause for which we are about to contend, and equally anxious with the rest of our fellow-subjects to promote that zeal which animates the breast of every Englishman to the preservation and defence of blessings that ought not to be lost but with existence, the non-commissioned officers and private soldiers of His Majesty's Egyptian brigade of Foot Guards, consisting of the first battalion of the Coldstream and the first battalion of the Third regiment, commanded by the Honourable Major-General Edward Finch, are desirous to subscribe from their weekly subsistence as follows, *viz*.: from the sergeants two full days' pay each; and from the corporals, drummers, and privates, one full day's pay each, amounting to £111. 5*s*. 7*d*., towards the support of the Patriotic Fund, now established for the relief of those who may eventually suffer in the prosecution of a contest, as glorious as it will no doubt be honourable, should the implacable enemy of our country

49

invade her shores.

In the name of the non-commissioned officers, drummers, and privates of the Egyptian brigade of Foot Guards,

Henry Selway, Sergeant-Major 1st Battalion Coldstream Guards.

Alexander Adams, Sergeant-Major 1st Battalion Third Guards.

In May, 1804, Cambaceres acquainted Buonaparte that it was the wish of the senate and of the people that he should accept the imperial dignity. Buonaparte consented to an arrangement which was so "essential to the welfare of the state," and was declared emperor on the twentieth of August. In the following December he was crowned by Pope Pius at Paris. The first battalions of the Coldstream and Third Guards marched from Chelmsford, July 24th, for Cox-Heath, where they encamped with several regiments of militia, under the Earl of Chatham.

★★★★★★

The corps encamped at Cox-Heath on the first of August, 1804:

23rd Light Dragoons

Coldstream Guards 1st Battalion.

Third Guard, 1st Battalion.

West York Militia. (First.)

     Do. Do. (Third.)

East York *Do.*

East Norfolk *Do.*

West *Do. Do.*

Bucks *Do.*

     —Quartermaster General's Office.

★★★★★★

On the first and second of November they went into November, barracks at Chatham, and remained there during the winter. April, 1805, the four flank companies from the Second Brigade of Guards at Chatham, and the six flank companies of the third brigade in London, marched to Windsor to attend the installation of the Garter. In May the first battalion marched from Chatham to, London, May 27th, 28th and 29th, and was reviewed at Wimbledon by His Majesty George the Third.

★★★★★★

Troops reviewed at Wimbledon by His Majesty King George the Third, June 14th, 1805. The brigade of Life Guards, one troop of Horse Artillery, one car-brigade of Artillery, right brigade of Foot Guards, left brigade of Foot Guards, a battalion of Light Infantry of Foot Guards, one car-brigade of Artillery, one troop of Horse Artillery, five squadrons of the Ninth Light Dragoons, five squadrons of the Fourteenth Light Dragoons.

★★★★★★

On the death of the Duke of Gloucester, June 14th, the Duke of York succeeded him in the command of the First regiment Guards and Sept. 5th, the Duke of Cambridge was appointed Colonel of the Coldstream. The Emperor of Austria had acceded to the treaty of Petersburgh on the ninth of August, Napoleon's plans for the invasion of England were consequently at an end, and the encampment of one hundred thousand men on the French coast was broken up. He declared to the senate his determination of immediately placing himself at the head of his army. The French at this time were on the Rhine, and consisted of seven corps, independent of the cavalry under the direction of Marshal Murat. The different corps were commanded by the following Marshals: Bernadotte, Davoust, Soult, Lannes, Ney, Augereau, and General Marmont.

Marshal Massena, with sixty thousand men under his orders, was in Italy, and. on reaching the Adige, had his forces increased by twenty thousand French under General Gouvion St. Cyr. The army of the Emperor of Germany consisted of three hundred thousand men in the most efficient state. The preparations of Russia were also on a great scale; her army amounted to upwards of one hundred and eighteen thousand men. The English, by way of a diversion in favour of Austria, equipped a force of twenty-six thousand men under Lord Cathcart. The first battalion of the Coldstream, commanded by Lieutenant-Colonel Thomas Armstrong, marched from Chatham on the thirtieth of August to Deal, and afterwards to Dover, (Oct, 9th), from which place they proceeded to Ramsgate, when they embarked, on October the 23rd.

They sailed from the Downs on the fourth of November, and, having landed at Cox-Haven on the 20th, marched to Bremen. Napoleon crossed the Rhine, and by the rapidity of his movements obliged the Austrians to act on the defensive. General Mack was hemmed in at Ulm and obliged to capitulate. Murat came up with General Werneck on the nineteenth of October, and after an engagement at Trachtelfingen the Austrian general capitulated. Marshal Massena, after a bloody contest at Coldiero, was beaten by the Archduke Charles.

Early in November, General Hillinger with an Austrian corps of five thousand men capitulated near Verona; he was made prisoner soon after the archduke commenced his retreat.

The French troops enteredVienna on the thirteenth of November. The Allies were forced by Napoleon to risk a general action, much against their own interest, as in a few days the third Russian Army was expected to join them. The Battle of Austerlitz commenced at the dawn of day and ended at night, on December the 2nd. The result of this action baffled the hopes of Austria, Russia, and England. In consequence of the victory gained by the French, the British troops returned from Bremen. February 23rd, 1806, the first battalion of the Coldstream disembarked at Ramsgate, and marched to Deal barracks.

Return of Officers of the 1st battalion Coldstream Guards.
October 23d, 1805.

Comp⁸.	Captains.		Lieutenants.	Ensigns.
Gren⁸.	Lieut.-Col. Henry Mac Kinnon	Capt⁸.	J. Thompson Henry Sullivan Chas. Maitland Christie	
	¹ Brig.-Gen. W. Wyn-yard	,,	Chas. Philips	Charles Doyle ² Matt. Fortescue
	Lt.-Col. T. Armstrong	,,	Lord A. Gordon	Thomas Wood John Freemantle
	,, ,, W. M. Pea-cocke	,,	Edwd. Dalling	³ Hon. G. Pelham George Bowles
	¹ Brig.-Gen. Wm. P. Acland	,,	Sir I. L. John-stone	Dan. Mac Kinnon Hon. Francis Hay Drummond
	Lt.-Col. W. H. Pringle	,,	R. Beckett	Hon. John Walpole Hon. Edward Boscawen
	,, ,, Matthew Lord Aylmer	,,	W. H. Raikes	Thomas Thoroton Thos. Barrow
	,, ,, Thos. Stibbert	,,	F. M. Sutton	H. W. Vachell W. Fairfield
	,, ,, Sir W. Sheridan	,,	George Smyth	Ed⁴. Jenkinson G. T. Baldwin
Light Infantry	,, ,, Richard Hulse	,,	Thos. Braddyll	
		,,	George Collier	
		,,	Charles Parker	

Adjutant, Captain Montague Wynyard.
Quarter-Master, John Holmes.
Surgeon, Charles Combe.
Assistant Surgeon, I. G. Mac Kenzie.
      ,,   ,,   Thomas Rose.

Absent on the Staff.

¹ { Brigadier-General Wm. Wynyard.
   ,,   ,,   Wm. P. Acland.
   Captain Edwd. Dalling.
    ,,   Ricd. Beckett.

² Absent. Recruiting.
³ Do. Sick.

Death of Moore

The Duke of York gave up the command of the regiment, May, 1807: at this period the officers of the Coldstream presented a vase to His Royal Highness as a testimony of their gratitude and attachment, which occasioned the following address, and reply:

Sir,

We the Officers of His Majesty's Coldstream Guards, impressed with the greatest respect and affection, beg leave to present to Your Royal Highness this vase, as a tribute of gratitude for the unremitted kindness and various instances of consideration and regard with which we have been favoured by Your Royal Highness during the long period we had the honour of serving under your immediate command as Colonel of the Regiment. Our fervent prayers are, that Your Royal Highness may long enjoy every happiness and blessing of life; and, as officers zealously devoted to our sovereign, and most affectionately to you, Sir, we trust our future services will ensure to us a continuance of those favourable sentiments, and of that protection, which it has so long a period been our pride and happiness to experience from Your Royal Highness.

To Field-Marshal

His Royal Highness the Duke of York.

Horse-Guards, 6th May, 1807

Gentlemen,

I receive with sentiments of the most heartfelt satisfaction this token of regard from the officers of the Coldstream Guards, and feel much indebted for the kindness with which you have expressed yourselves towards me.

I avail myself with great pleasure of this opportunity to assure you, that no colonel had ever greater inducements to be partial to a corps than I had during the long period I had the command of the regiment; as it was my happiness to find myself associated with men who equally claimed my esteem and affection in the civil capacities, as they were uniformly entitled to my approbation as officers.

Though not in the immediate command of the regiment, you may be assured, Gentlemen, that the Coldstream will ever retain my most ardent wishes for its honour and welfare, I am attached to the regiment by ties and considerations, the force of which no time can lessen; and in your happiness, individually and collectively, I shall ever feel the most lively interest.

    I am, &c.   Frederick.

Although the Duke of York quitted the command, he constantly entertained a strong predilection for the Coldstream, and continued through life to watch over its welfare with the greatest interest. Future historians will record the unwearied and successful efforts of His Royal Highness as Commander-in-Chief to ameliorate the character and condition of the British soldier; but in giving an account of the services of the Coldstream, it may be permitted here to remark, that the internal regulations, the discipline, and the respectability, for which it has been so much and so justly extolled, emanated in a great measure from this illustrious prince and amiable man.

The government of Denmark, which had hitherto observed a strict neutrality, influenced by France, prohibited all commerce with Great Britain; and an expedition, under Lord Cathcart and Admiral Gambier, was fitted out to prevent the Danish Navy from passing into the hands of the French. The brigade of Guards, under Major-General the Honourable Edward Finch, consisting of the first battalion of the Coldstream and first battalion of the Third Guards, embarked at Chatham, and arrived in Elsinore Roads on the ninth of August.

Return of the Officers of the 1st battalion of the Coldstream at Copenhagen, 1807.

	Captains.	* Lieutenants.	Ensigns.
Gren^{r.} Comp^{y.}	Lieut.-Col. H. Mac Kinnon	Capt. T. Thompson „ Sir H. Sullivan, "aide-de-camp to Major-Gen. the Hon. Ed^d. Finch" Capt. C. M. Christie	

	Major-General Lord Forbes, absent on the Staff at home	Capt. Chas. Philips	N. Dickenson Hon. T. Ashburnham
	Lieut.-Col. Thomas Armstrong	,, Thos. Wood	Wm. Lord Alvanley Ed^d. Noel Long
	Brig.-Gen. W. P. Acland, absent on the Staff at home	,, Hon. G. Pelham	Hon. F. H. Drummond George Bowles
	Lt.-Col. M. W. Peacocke	,, Thos. Braddyll, on the Staff	Hon. I. Walpole Peter Gaussen
	,, ,, William H. Pringle	,, George Smyth, on the Staff	Hon. W. G. Crofton Edwd. Harvey
	,, ,, Lord Aylmer	,, Edward Jenkinson	Wm. Burroughs Hon. Edwd. Boscawen
	,, ,, T. Stibbert	,, Edwd. Dalling	Dan. Mac Kinnon Chas. Gregory
	,, ,, Sir William Sheridan	,, Richard Beckett, Brigade-Major	Mat. Fortescue W. L. Walton
Light Comp^y.	,, ,, R. Hulse	,, Sir Gilbert Stirling ,, G. Collier ,, Thos. T. Barrow	

Adjutant, W. H. Raikes.
Quarter-Master, T. Holmes.
Battalion-Surgeon, C. Coombe.
Assistant, T. Mackenzie.
   ,, T. Rose.

All arrangements being completed for putting the men on shore, and the wind not allowing the transports to sail towards Copenhagen, it was determined to land halfway between Elsinore and that capital, at a village called Welbeck. At five o'clock on the morning of the sixteenth of August the troops got into the boats, and remained on the beach; towards the evening they commenced their march in three columns till night, when they halted till daybreak, and again marched for the purpose of investing the capital.

General Peyman, the Danish commander-in-chief, had previously sent to request passports for the king's nieces to proceed to Colding in Holstein. Soon after the brigade of Guards had entered the road to Copenhagen they were formed into line, and received the princesses with the honours due to their rank.

Lord Rosslyn with six thousand men from the Isle of Rugen joined the army, which now amounted to about twenty-seven thousand.

The Guards occupied the suburbs between Fredericksberg and the city; in their advance they were opposed by piquet of the enemy, which they dislodged. The British broke ground before Copenhagen on the eighteenth of August; after which the operations continued, notwithstanding frequent efforts to interrupt them on the part of the Danes. On the twenty-fourth the town was more closely invested; a summons was sent on the first of September, which not being complied with, the batteries opened next morning, and after a bombardment of three days, an armistice of twenty-four hours was proposed by the enemy for the purpose of preparing articles of capitulation. This delay was thought unnecessary; Lieutenant-Colonel Murray was instructed to intimate that no proposal could be listened to, unless accompanied by the unconditional surrender of the fleet. It was then agreed that the whole of the Danish Navy should be delivered up, and Zealand evacuated by the English within six weeks, or sooner if possible.

At four o'clock on the evening of the seventh the citadel was entered by Major-General Spencer's brigade.

No Englishman can desire to perpetuate the remembrance of this expedition, which laid the capital of a neutral state in ruins, and carried war and desolation among an innocent people. Its policy was doubtful, and its morality more than questionable, England indeed had reason to suspect, that the intention of Buonaparte was to compel the unfortunate Danes to unite their ships with his, as the price of their exemption from the ravages of his victorious troops, already threatening them. If ever a nation deserved commiseration, the Danes deserved it at that period: had they complied with the request of the English Government, and voluntarily given up their fleet to be carried to England for safe custody, the certain consequence would have been the subjugation of their country by the French armies.

In this disastrous predicament, an unoffending but feeble community were only allowed to choose between their political annihilation, and the bombardment of their chief city. They preferred the latter, were overpowered, and England carried off their ships in triumph; but they saved their national independence. Napoleon, had he retained his Imperial crown, would probably have thrown on England the onus of showing that he ever contemplated the appropriation of the Danish fleet to his own purposes. Unfortunately, the proofs of England's injustice are recorded in characters of blood: she was frightened for her safety, her magnanimity forsook her, and her fears made her cruel.

There is no reason to suppose that the addition of a few sail of the line would have transferred the superiority on the ocean to the fleets of the enemy, or that the expenses of the expedition might not have been better bestowed on the augmentation of the naval power of Great Britain, to enable her, after her suspicions were realised by the junction of the Danish men-of-war with those of France, to do that with honour which could only be dishonourably done while they remained dismantled in their own peaceful harbours. If the principle of making war by anticipation, without waiting for an overt act of hostility, be once admitted, there can be no repose or security among the nations of Europe; the existence of the false principle of anticipatory warfare will generate and justify fear, and fear will magnify danger.

It is far from the interest of the civilized world to multiply the causes of war, or that neutral nations should be subjected to fire and sword, their ships seized, their towns destroyed, their fields ravaged, and their crops annihilated by one belligerent to prevent the other from making use of them. The bombardment of Copenhagen, and the seizure of the Danish ships, were contrary to the most obvious principles of justice, and cannot even be vindicated on the treacherous plea of necessity; for at sea England ruled supreme: it was a fierce imitation of the ruthless, unhesitating policy of Napoleon.

The army began to re-embark on the thirteenth of October. and by the twentieth all had got on board; the and the Fourth regiment being the last that remained on shore.

The first battalion anchored in Yarmouth Roads, and then proceeded to Chatham, where they went into barracks.

March 19th, 1808, Charles the Fourth abdicated the throne of Spain in favour of his son Ferdinand; but soon after, in a letter to the French Emperor, he declared that it had been compulsory. In April Napoleon arrived at Bayonne, April 15th, ostensibly for the purpose of settling the differences among the Royal Family of Spain. Ferdinand, at the suggestion of the French ambassadors was induced, in opposition to the advice of his councillors, to meet him, April 20th. In Ferdinand's absence Murat entered Madrid at the head of a French Army: Godoy, Prince of Peace, who had been imprisoned, was released and sent under an escort, April 30th, to Bayonne. Charles the Fourth, with the queen, also repaired thither.

Napoleon had an interview with Charles, at which the Queen of Spain and Ferdinand were present. After Charles had accused Ferdinand of usurpation, and lavished on him the grossest abuse, and the queen had declared his illegitimacy, he was by threats and promises at last induced to sign a document renouncing all right and claim to the throne; and the other branches of the royal family were prevailed on to resign their pretensions in a similar manner. Charles the Fourth then ceded his claims in favour of Napoleon, Ferdinand, Don Antonio, his uncle, and his brother Don Carlos, fixed their residence at Valency. Charles, the Queen, and the Prince of Peace, retired to Rome.

Joseph Buonaparte was proclaimed King of Spain by an Imperial decree issued at Bayonne on the sixth of June. Ten days after this extraordinary event an insurrection broke out at Oporto, which spread with such rapidity through the northern provinces of Portugal that the French, who had taken possession of that country, were quickly expelled from it. The insurrection extended to Spain; and the French squadron at Cadiz was compelled to capitulate. Dupont's army of fifteen thousand men surrendered to the Spanish General Castanos. The patriots entered into a treaty with England. The Spanish troops in Denmark under the Marquis de la Romana succeeded in getting on board the British fleet, and conveyed to the Peninsula to assist their fellow-countrymen in opposing the usurpations of Napoleon.

On the twelfth of July a force of nine thousand three hundred and ninety-four men, commanded by Sir Arthur Wellesley, sailed from Cork: on clearing the coast the frigate in which he embarked left the fleet and steered for Corunna, where he had an interview with the provincial authorities, to whom he offered his co-operation. This was declined, on the ground that there was no immediate necessity for it in that quarter. Sir Arthur consequently sailed for Oporto, and held a conference with the bishop and other functionaries. From Oporto he proceeded off Lisbon: after communicating with Sir Charles Cotton, he returned, and commenced landing his troops in Mondego Bay on the first of August. General Spencer arrived on the sixth with reinforcements. The army then advanced.

On the seventeenth Sir Arthur Wellesley attacked the eights of Roliça with complete success, and on the twenty-first defeated the French under the Duke d'Abrantes at the Battle of Vimeira, which led to the evacuation of Portugal by the troops of Napoleon. (The enemy lost nearly three thousand men in the battle. Generals Foy and Thiebault, however, state the loss under two thousand.)

The French emperor returned to Paris on the October, eighteenth of October, and made known to the legislative body his determination to proceed in a few days for Madrid to place his brother Joseph on the Spanish throne. An army exceeding one hundred thousand men had already reinforced the French in that country.

The British troops in Sweden returned unexpectedly under Sir

John Moore, and were sent without delay to reinforce the army of Portugal.

Napoleon entered Madrid on the fourth of December, and issued a proclamation on the seventh. In which he declared that should the Spaniards prove themselves unworthy of his confidence, and resist his wishes, he had determined to treat them as a conquered province, give his brother another kingdom, and place the crown of Spain on his own head.

Napoleon quitted Madrid on the nineteenth, and put himself at the head of his troops for the purpose, as he boasted, of driving the British into the sea.

On the twentieth the troops under Sir John Moore and Sir David Baird formed a junction at Mayorga; four days after, that army commenced its disastrous retreat. This retrograde movement, necessary perhaps from circumstances, but rendered calamitous by insubordination and mismanagement, ended in the Battle of Corunna, January 16th, 1809. The British, on coming in contact with the enemy, recovered their discipline, and vigorously repulsed the French, who attacked in great force. But the triumph was clouded by the death of Sir John Moore, who was killed in the action.

This army embarked for England in the course of the night and following morning.

In the meantime, another expedition was prepared; and the brigade quartered at Chatham, under Brigadier-General Henry Campbell, composed of the first battalions of the Coldstream and Third Guards, marched to Ramsgate, (Dec. 27-30), where they went on board. During the night they anchored in the Downs, and proceeded next morning with other troops for Spithead. Major-General Sherbrooke was appointed to the command, January 1st, 1809.

Force which sailed under Major-General Sherbrooke :

	Lt.-Col.	Capt.	Sub.	Staff.	Rk. & File.	Wom.	Commanded.
1st Bat. Colds. Gds.	7	7	14	5	1120	17	Lt.-Col. Hulse
1st Bat. 3d Guards	7	14	16	5	1361	19	Col. Hon. E. Stopford
	14	21	30	8	2481	36	Brig.-Gen. Campbell
	Major.						
87th Foot	2	6	23	6	791	15	Major Gough
88th Foot	2	8	25	6	842	22	Lt.-Col. Duff
	4	14	48	12	1633	57	Major-Gen. Tilson
Total	14 5	34	78	20	4114	73	

Lt.-Col. Lord Aylmer, Dy.-Adj. General.
Col. Burke, Dy.-Qr. Mas.-General.
Mr. Boys, Pay-Master-General.
Dr. Somers, Principal Medical Officer.

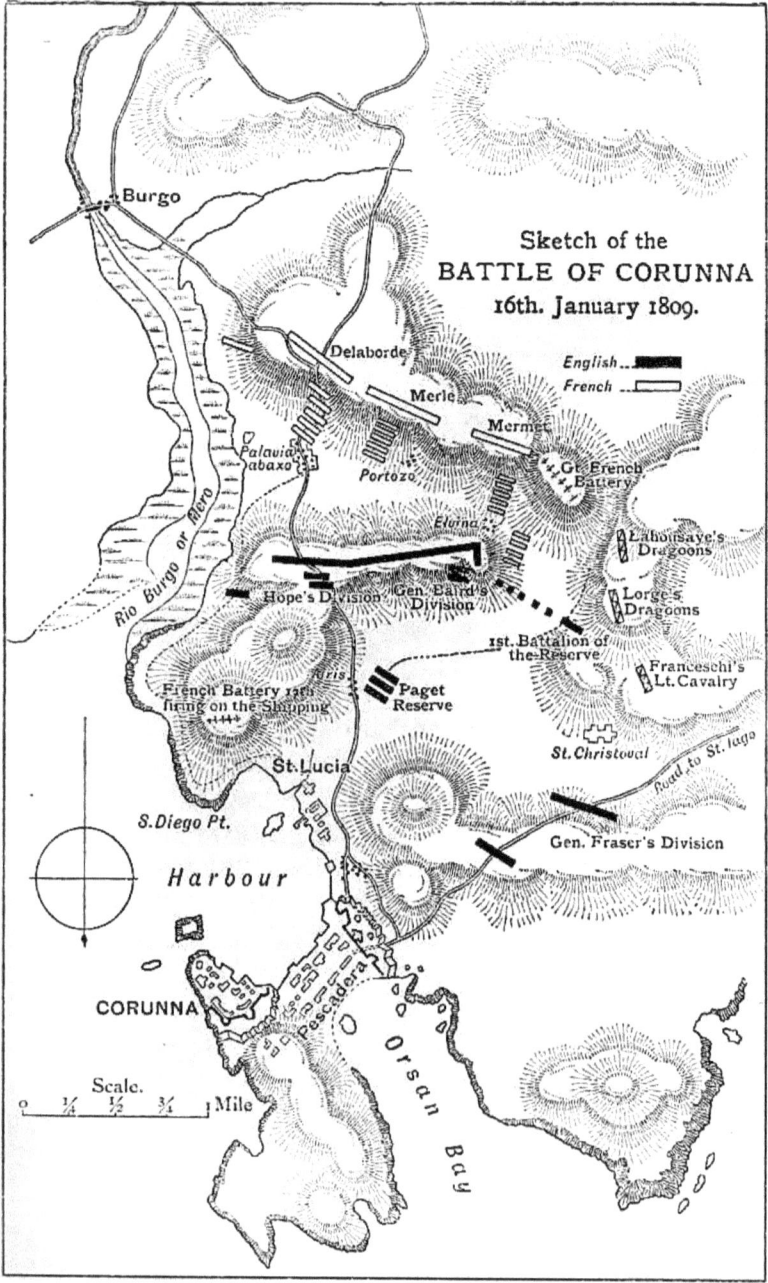

Sketch of the
BATTLE OF CORUNNA
16th. January 1809.

English ___
French ___

Burgo

Delaborde

Merle

Mermet

Palavia abaxo

Portozo

Gt. French Battery

Elvina

Lahoussaye's Dragoons

Hope's Division

Gen. Baird's Division

Lorge's Dragoons

1st. Battalion of the Reserve

Franceschi's Lt. Cavalry

French Battery firing on the Shipping

Iris

Paget Reserve

St. Christoval

Rio Burgo or Mero

Road to St. Iago

St. Lucia

S. Diego Pt.

Gen. Fraser's Division

Harbour

CORUNNA

Pescadera

Orsan Bay

Scale.
0   ¼   ½   ¾   1 Mile

The fleet sailed on the fifteenth of January, and encountered a series of contrary and tempestuous winds. On the thirtieth the ships were dispersed in a tremendous gale, when most of the transports took shelter in the Cove of Cork.

The expedition sailed again on the twenty-fifth of February, and proceeded direct for Cadiz, in the hope of securing that important sea-port.

The Supreme Junta, however, refused the troops admittance, stating as an excuse, that the confidence of the Spaniards in their allies was at an end. General Sherbrooke perceiving that further negotiation would only be attended with loss of time, proceeded for the Tagus, and the defence of Portugal then became the primary object of Great Britain.

★★★★★★

During the night of the ninth of March the *Prince George* transport, headquarter ship of the Coldstream Guards, ran down an American brig, the crew of which, with the exception of one man, was saved; when the *Isis*, of fifty guns, coming to their assistance, got foul of the *Prince George*, whose mizen-mast was carried away; and it being supposed the transport must sink, the captain and forty men got on board the *Isis*. Unfortunately, Ensign Edward Noel Long, one drummer, and one private, were lost.

★★★★★★

Major-General Beresford was appointed Commander in-Chief of the Portuguese levies, with the rank of marshal in their service. He was perfectly qualified for the situation, and employed himself with the greatest zeal and activity in re-modelling the Portuguese Army, which, previous to his command, had been in the lowest state of degradation.

This general introduced subordination, and convinced them of the advantages arising from discipline. English officers were placed in command of regiments, and a regular organisation established. Nine companies of the first battalion of the Coldstream, after landing, March 13th, occupied the barracks at Belem, and on the twenty-second marched to Saccavem, where they remained till April.

★★★★★★

The light company of the Coldstream had been driven into the Waterford River by the gales which occurred at the end of January; from Waterford they proceeded to the Cove of Cork, and joined the expedition under Major-General Hill, and only

landed at Belem (under the command of Lieut.-Colonel Fuller) on the sixth of April: they marched next day for the purpose
of joining the first battalion.

★★★★★★

The British force in Portugal, under the command of Lieutenant-
General Sir J. Cradock, amounted to about eighteen thousand men,
besides twenty thousand native troops taken into British pay. In addition to these, fresh levies were raised in all parts, and the inhabitants
now looked forward with confidence to the successful defence of
their country.

Soult had crossed the Minho on the twenty-seventh of February, and shortly after completely defeated the Spaniards under the
Marquis de la Romana, near Monterry. The French marshal after this
exploit crossed the Minho, and marched on Oporto, (French bulletins
announced Soult's army would reach Oporto on the twentieth of
March, and arrive at Lisbon by the end of the month), which was carried by assault, capturing nearly fifteen hundred prisoners, although
defended by a force of twenty thousand irregular troops, and a line of
works extending from the Douro to the sea, on which were mounted
two hundred guns. At the capture of this place a dreadful scene of
carnage ensued.

The Portuguese General Silveira retook Chaves, March 20th (they
are said to have lost ten thousand men), and also rendered an essential
service in cutting off Soult's communication with Spain, and securing
the bridge of Amarante

The Guards marched from Saccavem, April 9th, through Batalha,
to Lyria, where Sir John Cradock resigned the command of the army
to Sir Arthur Wellesley, who arrived at Lisbon on the twenty-second
of April.

Adjutant-General's Office,
Lisbon, 27thApril, 1809.

General Order,

His Majesty has been pleased to appoint Lieutenant-General
Sir Arthur Wellesley, K.B. to be Commander of his Forces in
Portugal; and his Excellency having arrived in this country to
assume the command all reports, applications, &c. are hencefor-
ward to be addressed to him through the usual channels.

His Excellency having appointed the following officers to be
his *aides-de-camp*, they are to be obeyed accordingly.

Lieut.-Col. Bathurst, 60th Foot, Military Secretary.

Captain the Hon. Fitzroy Stanhope, 1st Guards, ⎫
   ,,   Lord Fitzroy Somerset, 43d Foot, ⎪
   ,,   Henry Bouverie, Coldm Guards, ⎬ Aides-de-Camp.
   ,,   George Canning, 3d Guards, ⎭

STAFF OF THE FORCES IN PORTUGAL.

Lieut.-Gen. Sir Arthur Wellesley, K.B. Commander of the Forces.

Major-Gen. Sherbrooke, ⎫ With the local rank of Lieut.-
   ,,   Payne, ⎪ Generals in Portugal during
   ,,   Lord W. Bentinck ⎬ the continuance of this ser-
   ,,   Paget, ⎭ vice.

Major-Gen. Cotton.	Major-Gen. Erskine.
,, Hill.	,, McKenzie.
,, Murray.	,, Tilson.
Brig.-Gen. A. Campbell.	Brig.-Gen. H. Fane.
,, H. Campbell.	,, Drieberg.
,, R. Stewart.	,, Langworth.
,, A. Cameron.	

Colonel Donkin, Colonel on the Staff.

ADJUTANT GENERAL'S DEPARTMENT.

Brigadier-Genl. the Hon. Charles Stewart, Adjutant-General.

Lieut.-Col. Darrock, 36th Regiment, ⎫
  ,,   ,, Lord Aylmer, Coldm. Guards, ⎪
Bt.-Lt.-Col. Hinuber, 68th Foot, ⎪
Lt.-Col. John Elley, R. Regt. Horse Guards, ⎬ Assist.-Adjutant-
Major F. S. Tidy, 14th Foot, ⎪ Generals.
Bt.-Major Williamson, 30th do. ⎪
Major Geo. Berkeley, 35th do. ⎪
Major Colin Campbell, 70th do. ⎭

  Captain Willoughby Cotton, 3rd Guards, ⎫
    ,,   John Elliott, 48th Foot, ⎪
    ,,   Charles Dashwood, 3rd Guards, ⎬ Deputy-Asst.-Adjt.-
    ,,   Francis Cockburn, 60th Foot, ⎪ Generals.
    ,,   Vernon Graham, 26th do. ⎪
    ,,   Henry Mellish, 87th do. ⎭

Lieut. George During, 1st Battn K.G.L. is attached to this Department until further orders.

QUARTER-MASTER-GENERAL'S DEPARTMENT.

Colonel George Murray, 3rd Guards, Quarter-Master-General.

Lieut.-Colonel Wm. Delancey, Perm. Staff,
    ,,   ,,   James Bathurst, 60th Foot,
    ,,   ,,   R. Bourke, Perm. Staff,
Major George de Blaquiere,   do.
  ,, Augustus Northey,   do.
} Assistant-Quarter-Master-Generals.

Captain Matthew Sutton, 97th Foot,
   ,,   Algernon Langton, 61st do.
   ,,   Dawson Kelly, 27th do.
   ,,   J. Haverfield, 48th do.
   ,,   George Scovell, 57th do.
   ,,   Robert Waller, 103rd do.
   ,,   William Beresford, 8th Gn. Bn.
} Deputy-Ass¹.-Quarter-Master-Generals.

MEDICAL DEPARTMENT.

A. Thompson, Inspector of Hospitals.

———— Bolton, Deputy Inspector of Hospitals.

C. Larchin
E. Somers
} Physicians {
———— Buchan.

J. F. Nicholay
———— Morrel
J. Forbes
L. Kraziesur
} Staff Surgeons {
A. Bole
S. Higgins
H. Irwin
J. Cooke.

William Williams
William Graham
} Apothecaries.

R. Matthews, Acting Apothecary.

W. H. O'Reily, Deputy Purveyor.

24 Hospital Mates.

COMMISSARIAT DEPARTMENT.

John Murray, Esq. Commissary-General.

Charles Dalrymple, Deputy-Commissary-General.

Rawlings
Boys
Dunmore
} Acting Deputy-Commissary-General.

Honeyman
O'Meara
Pratt
Murray
Gauntlett
} Assistant Commissary {
Young
Dillon
Grieve
Aylmer
Mc Kenzie.

	Acting-Assistant-Commissary	
Coffin		Mc Donnell
Hodges		Smidchin
Pelken		Moore
Belson		Strahan
Nelson		Haden
Joly		Melville
De Bels		Dick
Ogilvie		Gordon
Downie		Brooke
Haines		Maude.

Previous to this time Marshals Soult and Victor had agreed to proceed to Lisbon, the former by Coimbra, the latter by Abrantes; but this plan was not carried into execution.

The brigade of Guards marched into Coimbra on the first of May, where they were received with shouts of joy; the balconies were filled with females; embroidered and damask cloths, as is customary in Catholic countries on great festivals, were suspended from the windows; sweetmeats, sugar-plums, and orange flowers, were showered on the soldiers in great profusion during their passage through the town: in the evening the city was illuminated.

Colonel Trant was stationed in fronts holding the line of the Vouga with two thousand irregular troops, of which three hundred were students from the University. This position he kept against the enemy until the advance of the British on the tenth.

CHAPTER 6

Battle of Talavera

Sir Arthur Wellesley arrived on the second of May, 1809, at Coimbra, and advanced against Oporto on May 6th, after reviewing his
army, which consisted of twenty-five thousand men, including three
thousand Germans and nine thousand Portuguese.

Beresford was ordered with the Portuguese to intercept Soult if he
should attempt to retreat by Amarante. General Hill with his division
embarked on the ninth at Aveiro to turn the enemy's right. The rest
of the army under Sir Arthur moved by the direct road to Oporto,
On the eleventh the French were dislodged from a range of hills on
which they were strongly posted at Grijon. They retreated and entered Oporto during the night, after which the bridge of boats was re
moved, being the only bridge over the Douro at that place.

Soon after seven a.m. on the twelfth the British marched through
Villa Nova, and halted on the heights opposite Oporto, which was
effected without their columns being exposed to view. The enemy
had neglected to guard the river above the town, not expecting any
attempt would be made in that direction. After a few boats were collected higher up, at a bend in the Douro, out of sight of the enemy's
piquets, Major-General Paget crossed with the Buffs, and was followed by the rest of Major-General Hill's brigade.

They took possession of a building which was maintained in spite
of every effort of the French to dislodge them; here General Paget
lost his arm. Several guns were planted near the convent of Sarea in
Villa Nova to support the attack. Major-General Murray with his brigade and some cavalry crossed at Barca d'Avintas, a few miles higher
up. The Guards then advanced to the water-side through Villa Nova,
where the river was upwards of three hundred yards broad, very deep,
and extremely rapid. They crossed at two o'clock p.m. in boats at the

spot where the bridge, prior to its removal, had been placed, (the light infantry of the Coldstream were the first that passed over to the town); and, on landing, were immediately sent in pursuit.

They charged the right of the French, and drove them through the principal streets, taking many prisoners and baggage. The enemy's left was endangered by the appearance of the brigade under Major-General Murray. The rest of the British crossed as quickly as the boats could convey them. The Guards, while driving the French through the streets, were everywhere received by the inhabitants in the same manner as at Coimbra. Amidst the conflict the soldiers were encouraged with enthusiastic cheers; "*Viva os Inglezes*," *Viva Grand Britania,*" "*Viva O Grand Wellington*," resounded on all sides. Hogsheads of wine were brought into the streets and given to the troops, and blessings were universally bestowed by the inhabitants on the brave English who had so gallantly relieved them from their cruel oppressors.

Soult's loss must have been very considerable: his army left the place in complete disorder; they were undoubtedly surprised, and, according to the statements of the in habitants, had thought themselves perfectly secure.

The passage of the Douro was one of the most gallant and brilliant exploits that had taken place for a series of years. The English general crossed this broad and rapid river at midday, with only a few boats, in the face of an active and skilful enemy. Although the city of Oporto was defended by one of the ablest Marshals of France, commanding troops unused to defeat, this victory was achieved with a loss on the part of the British not exceeding one hundred and twenty-five killed and wounded.

When the pursuit was over the brigade of Guards returned to Oporto, and were quartered in the Rue d'Almeida,

After congratulating the army on their success, Sir Arthur Wellesley thus alludes to the conduct of the Guards in the General Order.

Oporto, 12 May, 1809.—The timely passage of the Douro, and subsequent movement on the enemy's flank by lieutenant-General Sherbrooke with the brigade of Guards and 29th regiment, and the bravery of the two squadrons of the 14th Light Dragoons under the command of Major Harvey, and led by Brigadier General Charles Stewart, obtained the victory which has contributed so much to the honour of the troops on this day.

The situation of Soult's army was critical; having learnt at Penafiel that Beresford had obliged Loison to quit the ground he occupied on the Tamega, Soult determined to march on Guimaraens; to effect which he abandoned his guns, ammunition, military chest, baggage, and took to the paths across the mountains, leaving Braga on the left. By this manoeuvre he gained a day in advance.

★★★★★★

This fine city of Braga, had been plundered, and everything valuable or ornamental had been destroyed. The retreat of the French was everywhere marked by burning villages, and inconceivable wretchedness of the inhabitants.

★★★★★★

Sir Arthur left Oporto on the fourteenth, and arrived at Braga next day, where the troops were received with the same enthusiasm as at Coimbra and Oporto. On the sixteenth the British moved from Braga, and came on the rear-guard of the French Army, which was strongly posted at Salamonde. The enemy's right was protected by a deep ravine; the road as far as the village was exposed to the fire of their position: their left was covered by an extremely high hill. Two companies of the Coldstream under Colonel Henry Mackinnon crowned the height, for the purpose of turning the enemy's left: on their appearance the brigade of Guards was ordered to advice.

This attack was led by the light companies of the Coldstream and Third Guards, with the Sixtieth Rifles, under the command of Lieutenant-Colonel Fuller of the Coldstream. After firing a volley, the enemy fled in great confusion. Two or three guns were brought to bear on the bridge of Ponte Nova, over which they endeavoured to escape, though not in the direct road of retreat; and at this spot great numbers were killed, many were crushed, others fell over the bridge, which had no parapet, and were drowned. Sir Arthur Wellesley, in his dispatch, dated Monte Alegre, May the eighteenth, 1809, says:

The brigade of Guards were at the head of the column, and set a laudable example; and in the affair with the enemy's rear-guard on the evening of the sixteenth they conducted themselves remarkably well.

The French continued their retreat, and on the eighteenth the Coldstream crossed the bridge at Ruvaens, and halted, after a long march, at Scavessa de Rio, in the Sierra Gerres, where they remained the next day, and the pursuit terminated.

The British returned through Braga to Oporto, which they reached on the twenty-fourth. This town they left on the twenty-eighth, and arrived at Coimbra on the third of June; they then continued their route through Lyria and Thomar to Abrantes, near which place the army concentrated. The arrangements of the army were as follows on quitting Abrantes:

CAVALRY.	COMMANDING OFFICERS.			
3d Dragoon Guards,	Sir Granby Calcraft	Brig.-Gen. Fane		Lt.-Gen. Payne.
4th Dragoons,	Lord Ed. Somerset			
14th Lt. Dragoons,	Lt.-Col. Hawker	Maj.-Gen. Cotton		
16th do.	Maj.-Hon. L. Stanhope			
23d do.'	Col. Seymour	Maj.-Gen. Erskine		
1st do. K. G. Leg.	Baron Alten			
Artillery	Col. Robe ,, Framingham	Maj.-Gen. Howarth.		
1st batt. Coldst. Gds.	Lt.-Col. Hulse	Brig.-Gen. Campbell		1st Division, Maj.-Gen. Sherbrooke.
1st batt. 3d Gds.	Col. Hon. E. Stopford			
40th regiment		Brig.-Gen. Cameron		
83d do.	Lt.-Col. Gordon			
60th, one company				
1st reg. K. G. Legion,	Major Bodecker	Brig.-Gen. Langworth		
2d do. do.				
Light inf. five comps.				
5th reg. K. G. Legion,	Major Gerber	Brig.-Gen. Lowe		
7th do. do.	Major Berger			
Light inf. five comps.				
3d reg. Buffs,	Lt.-Col. Muter	Brig.-Gen. Tilson		2d Division, Maj.-Gen. Hill.
66th do. 2d batt.	Capt. Kelley			
60th, one company				
1st batt. detachments,	Lt.-Col. Bunbury	Brig.-Gen. R. Stewart		
29th reg.	,, White			
45th reg. 1st batt.	Lt.-Col. Guard	Maj.-Gen. McKenzie		3d Division.
24th do.	Col. Drummond			
60th, one company		Colonel Donkin		
87th, 2d batt.	Major Rose			
88th, 1st batt.	Major Vandeleur			

69

7th reg. 2d batt.	Sir Wm. Myers	} Brig.-Gen. Campbell	} 4th Division.
53d do. do.			
60th, one company			
2d batt. detachments,	L⁴.-Col. Copson	} Brig.-Gen. Anson	
97th reg. ,,	L⁴.-Col. Lyon		
60th, one company			

STAFF.

Major-General Sherbrooke

,,   ,,   Payne } Local rank of

,,   ,,   Lord Wm. Bentinck { Lieutenant-Generals.

,,   ,,   ,,   Paget

Major-Gen. Cotton.	Brig.-Gen. A. Campbell.
,, Hill.	,, H. Campbell.
,, Erskine.	,, R. Stewart.
,, M⁣ᶜKenzie.	,, Cameron.
,, Tilson.	,, Fane.
	,, Anson.
	,, Langworth, K. G. L.
	,, Lowe, K. G. L.

Col. Donkin on the Staff.

Adj⁴-Gen¹ Hon. C. Stewart.

Q⁴-Master-Gen¹ Col. George Murray.

The Ninety-Fifth, Fifty-Second, and Forty-Third regiments, under General Craufurd, from England, and the Forty-Eighth and Sixty-First regiments from Gibraltar, were at Lisbon on their way to join the army. Sir Arthur Wellesley now determined to commence operations in Spain.

★★★★★★

The British troops under Sir Arthur Wellesley amounted to about nineteen thousand infantry and one thousand five hundred cavalry. Romana with fifteen thousand men was in Gallicia; and Blake with about twenty thousand was in Valencia; Beresford, with twelve thousand Portuguese and ten thousand Spaniards, under the Duke del Parque, was to watch Soult; and the pass of Banos was to be guarded to prevent Soult advancing to Placentia.

★★★★★★

The French under Victor, amounting to upwards of twenty thousand men, were on the Tagus: Sebastiani's corps, not quite so numerous, were in La Mancha: several thousand men were quartered in and about Madrid. Marshals Soult, Ney, and Mortier, with a large force, were in Old Castile, Gallicia, and Leon: besides which there were a division of cavalry, and forty thousand men stationed in Arragon, Catalonia, and the adjacent country.

The allies marched from Abrantes on June 27th, by Salvatierra, on Placentia, July 12th. They left Placentia on the seventeenth of July, formed a junction with General Cuesta's army at Oropesa, and moved in two columns on Talavera de la Reyna; from whence Marshal Victor, after making a slight resistance, retired across the Alberche.

The most positive assurances had been given by the Spanish Government to Sir Arthur Wellesley that his army should be regularly supplied with provisions and means of transport during his advance; but, either from neglect on the part of the proper authorities, or from the exhausted state of the country, these promises were not fulfilled. In consequence the troops underwent great privations. (An officer of the Coldstream gave a dollar for a small loaf on the day preceding the Battle of Talavera.) Sir Arthur refused to move, and even threatened to return to Portugal if the rations and means of conveyance so frequently demanded and promised were not forthcoming.

The Spanish general, Cuesta, advanced to Santa Olalla, he was there attacked, and retreated in great disorder to the Alberche, where his troops joined the British. The position of the Allies occupied nearly two miles. July 27th, the Spaniards were strongly posted on the right in front of Talavera, extending to the Tagus; here they were sheltered from the fire of the French guns, and the space was intersected with ditches, mud enclosures, olive trees, and vineyards. The centre of the line was more open. The left was on a lofty ascent, and a ravine ran along the front. The communication from the hill with the rest of the English line was of easy and gradual descent.

This height was at first occupied only by Colonel Donkin's brigade, who, being unable to defend so large a space, had his left turned; he was reinforced by General Hill, when the enemy were driven from the summit. Soon after dark an attempt was made to dislodge the German Legion, which however maintained its ground. About the same time a fire commenced from the left of the British line, which was taken up by the Guards, and partially went down the brigade: from this unfortunate occurrence. Lieutenant-Colonel Ross, Captain Bryan, and two men were killed. In this conflict the British loss amounted to eight

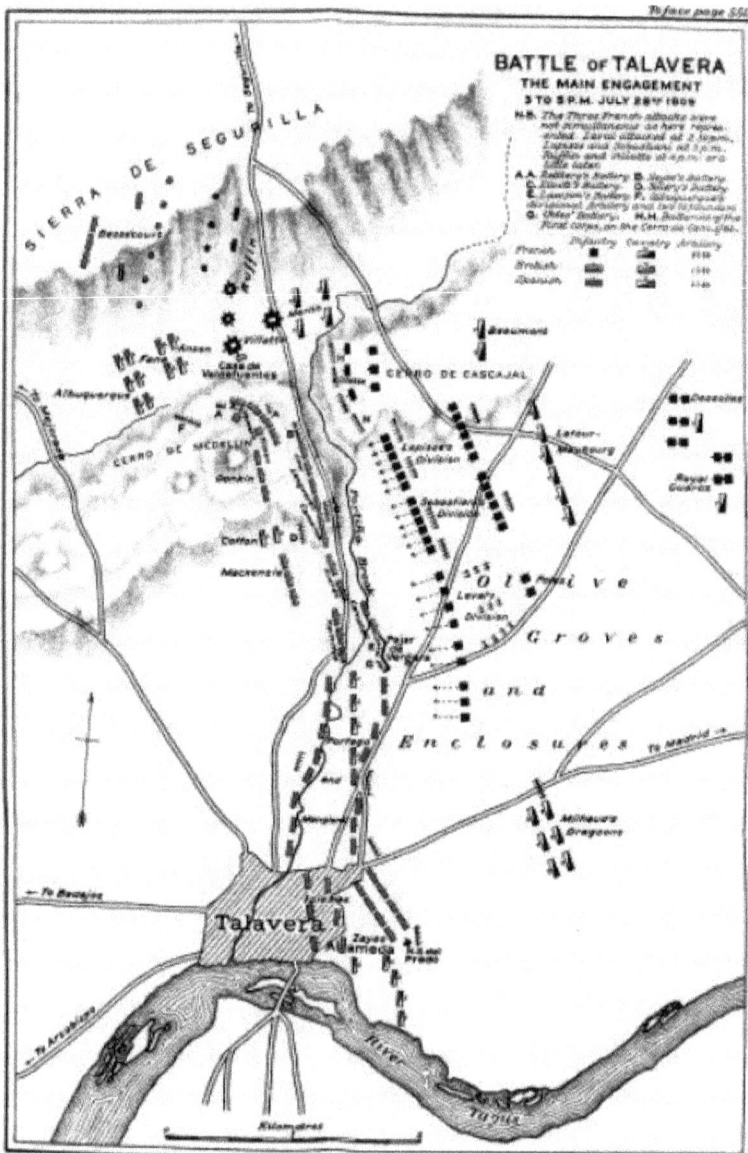

BATTLE of TALAVERA
THE MAIN ENGAGEMENT
3 TO 5 P.M. JULY 28TH 1809

N.B. The Three French attacks were
not simultaneous as here repre-
sented. Laval attacked at 2 p.m.,
Lapisse and Sebastiani at 3 p.m.,
Ruffin and Villatte at 4 p.m.; are
little later.

A.A. Rettberg's Battery B. Heyse's Battery
C. Elliott's Battery D. Sillery's Battery
E. Lawson's Battery F. Gardiner's
G. Chles' Battery Disposed Artillery and left to advance
H.H. Bottom of the
First corps, on the Cerro de Cascajal.

Infantry   Cavalry   Artillery

French
British
Spanish

SIERRA DE SEGURILLA

Bassecourt

Villatte

Anson

Fane

Casa de Valdefuentes

Albuquerque

Beaumont

CERRO DE CASCAJAL

Lapisse's
Division

Lafour-
Bourg

CERRO DE MEDELLIN

Donkin

Cotton

Macckenzie

Sebastiani's
Division

O l i v e

Leval's
Division

G r o v e s

a n d

E n c l o s u r e s

To Madrid

Burgos

Milhaud's
Dragoons

To Bazajos

Talavera

To Arzobispo

Zayas
Alameda

Prado

River Tagus

Kilometres

hundred; that of the French was estimated at one thousand.

At daylight, July 28th, two strong columns, supported by a third, under a discharge of artillery, advanced against the left of the British position. This attack was conducted with great order; the French moved on at a quick pace, crossed the ravine, and mounted the ascent, where they were received by the brigades of Tilson and Richard Stewart, A destructive fire of musketry was well kept up on both sides; but the assailants were at length thrown into disorder, and retired to their original ground. During the attack General Hill, who commanded on the left, was wounded.

The roll of the French drums was distinctly heard at one o'clock, and the enemy were again seen in motion through clouds of dust. About two the French light troops advanced; four dense columns followed them, covered by eighty guns. The English, notwithstanding the heavy loss they sustained from the cannonade, patiently reserved their fire till the near approach of the enemy.

General Sebastiani almost reached the redoubt on the right of the British; but the troops commanded by Brigadier-General Alexander Campbell, with two Spanish battalions, drove them back with great slaughter, taking thirteen pieces of cannon.

On the left, Brigadier-General Anson with the Twenty-Third, and First German Hussars, was ordered to charge the head of Villatte's column. When at the gallop, the brigade was suddenly checked by a deep ravine. The Twenty-Third Light Dragoons, in defiance of the fire from the squares, dashed heedlessly on, passed between the divisions of Ruffin and Villatte, and charged a brigade of *chasseurs*. A body of cavalry sent by Marshal Victor coming up, the regiment was surrounded, broken, and nearly annihilated.

The centre, occupied by Sherbrooke's division, on the approach of the column under Lapisse was in readiness to charge. The French advanced with great resolution under the protection of their numerous artillery. They were received with calm intrepidity by the first division, who discharged a volley, and rushed on them with irresistible impetuosity. The brigade of Guards pursued the enemy so far as to expose itself to be attacked by the reserve columns, and taken in flank by the fire of the artillery. The French cavalry also advanced, and the brigade suffered very severely: about six hundred in a few minutes were killed and wounded, and its entire destruction appeared inevitable.

The first battalion of the Forty-Eighth regiment (commanded by two gallant officers, Lieutenant-Colonel Donelan and Major

Middlemore,the latter taking the command when the former fell), and Major-General Cotton's cavalry, were ordered to their support, when the Guards rallied, and again heroically advanced with renewed huzzas to the aid of the gallant Forty-Eighth. These cheers were echoed along the whole of the British line! It was the shout of triumph! The French were beaten; and although some skirmishing was kept up by the light troops, and occasionally a heavy cannonade, they retired to their original position.

★★★★★★

The British lost about five thousand three hundred and sixty-seven men, amongst whom were Major-Generals McKenzie and Langworth. The loss of the French may be calculated at between eight and ten thousand. The loss of the Spaniards, according to their own statement, was twelve hundred. Seventeen guns were captured by the English.

List of officers of the Coldstream Guards killed and wounded at Talavera, 27th and 28th July, 1809.

Lieutenant-Colonel Ross, Captain Beckett, and Ensign Parker killed: Lieutenant-Colonels Stibbert, Sir W. Sheridan, Captains Bouverie, Collier, Milman, Christie, Wood, Jenkinson, Bryan, and Ensign Sandilands, wounded.

Captains Jenkinson and Bryan (Adjutant) died of wounds.

Killed—3 officers & 33 rank and file

Wounded—10 officers, 11 sergeants. 1 drummer & 241 rank and file.

★★★★★★

In the evening of the twenty-eighth the grass, which was very long and dry, ignited, and the fire spread with such rapidity, that several of the wounded were burnt to death. During the night the men lay on their arms, and suffered greatly from the want of provisions. Next morning a rear guard of cavalry was all that was visible of the French Army. The following appeared in General Orders, dated Talavera de la Reyna, July twenty-ninth, 1809.

The charge made by the brigade of Guards under the command of Brigadier-General Henry Campbell, on the enemy's attacking column, was a most gallant one.

The light brigade, consisting of a troop of horse-artillery, the Forty-Third, Fifty-Second, and Ninety-Fifth Rifles, under Major-General Robert Craufurd, joined, after marching sixty-two miles in twenty-six hours in the hottest weather, leaving only seventeen stragglers on the road.

Soult having forced the strong passes between Salamanca and Placentia, Sir Arthur Wellesley resolved that the British Army should immediately march to Oropesa, (Aug, 3rd), leaving the Spanish General Cuesta to remain in position at Talavera.

Notwithstanding this arrangement, Cuesta left his position without the knowledge of Sir Arthur Wellesley, and joined him with his army at daylight on the fourth, having marched all night. In so doing Cuesta abandoned the sick and wounded of the British Army, amounting to five thousand men, who had been left at Talavera under the command of Colonel Henry Mackinnon of the Coldstream Guards. As Marshal Victor was only a few leagues distant. Colonel Mackinnon had received instructions in case of necessity to make the best of his way to Merida by the bridge of Arzobispo. When he saw Cuesta marching away, he applied to that general for transport, and it was with great difficulty he could procure half a dozen bullock cars, Colonel H. Mackinnon, who wrote and spoke the French language remarkably well, obtained for those unfortunate men, whom there was no possibility of removing, the most humane and honourable treatment.

★★★★★★

Marshal Victor arrived at Talavera on the seventh. His advance (Fifth Chasseurs) took possession of Talavera on the sixth. The following officers of the Coldstream were taken prisoners:— Lieutenant-Colonel Sir William Sheridan, Captains Christie, Milman, and Bryan; Ensign Sandilands, and Assistant-Surgeon Whymper.

★★★★★★

After parading all those that were able to move, at three o'clock in the afternoon of the third he set out on his march to Calera. The following day he joined the British at Arzobispo, and forty more cars were added to his means of transport; but these were in so bad a state, that having to cross the worst roads in the world, only eleven of them reached Deleytosa. Colonel H. Mackinnon nevertheless marched about two thousand sick and wounded soldiers from Talavera to Elvas, a distance of fifty-one leagues, without any assistance from the local authorities, and with only one commissary's clerk to furnish them with food. During his march, the inhabitants frequently evinced feelings of hostility, and he was compelled to resort to coercive measures to preserve his men from starvation.

★★★★★★

The wounded taken prisoners in the hospitals of Talavera were six lieutenant-colonels, three majors, sixteen captains, thirty-two lieutenants, eleven ensigns, two thousand rank and file; all in charge of one staff-surgeon and twenty-one assistant-surgeons.

★★★★★★

Sir Arthur Wellesley crossed the Tagus at Arzobispo; Cuesta followed, leaving the Duke del Albuquerque with a considerable force to defend the bridge, and withdrawing the remainder of his army to Paraleda de Garben. The French having succeeded in fording the river, not more than two hundred yards above the bridge, surprised the Spaniards, and took their works in rear. On this occasion Albuquerque charged with great determination; but fresh troops came up, which obliged the Spaniards to retreat, with the loss of thirty guns, ammunition, and baggage. Cuesta retired to Deleytosa, and the British fell back from that place to Zaraicejo.

It was found impossible to supply the troops with provisions; and as all concert between Cuesta and Sir Arthur was at an end, the latter resolved to establish his headquarters at Badajoz.

The brigade of Guards reached Merida on the twenty-fourth of August, and remained there till the beginning of September; they afterwards, on the third, marched towards Talavera Real. Whilst they were in this neighbourhood hats were constructed to protect the men from the heat, which was excessive. The brigade entered Badajoz on the tenth of October.

General Order, dated Badajoz, September 24, 1809.
The Commander of the Forces deems it but justice to the two battalions of Guards to state, that their returns have in every respect been as accurate as the conduct of those excellent corps has been regular and exemplary in every other respect.

War had been declared on the sixth of April between France and Austria Napoleon quitted Paris in that month to take the field. Marshal Davoust was with a French corps at Ratisbon, Massena at Ulm, Oudinot at Augsburg. Headquarters at Strasburg.

The Bavarians, under Le Fevre, Generals Roy and Wrede, were at Munich, Landshut, and Staubing. A division of Wirtemburgers was at Hydenheim, The Saxons were encamped at Dresden, and Ponia-

76

towski's corps was under the walls of Warsaw,

Napoleon gained the Battle of Abensberg on the twentieth, where he overthrew two corps commanded by the Archduke Lewis and General Hillier; the day after, he gained another victory at Landshut. On the twenty-second he attacked the Archduke Charles at Eckmuhl, and forced the latter to retire behind the Danube with great loss. (The Austrians lost about two thousand prisoners, with part of their artillery. According to the French accounts, forty thousand were taken prisoners, besides one hundred pieces of cannon.)

To create a diversion in favour of Austria, a formidable expedition was prepared by England for invading the French dominions. About the end of July forty thousand men were collected: a fleet of thirty-nine sail of the line, with thirty-six frigates, besides a vast number of gunboats, bomb-vessels, and other small craft, was fitted out. The object of this armament was the occupation of Flushing, and the destruction of the French ships, arsenals, and dock-yards at Antwerp. The command of the expedition was entrusted to Lord Chatham. The fleet was under Sir Richard Strachan, and sailed in two divisions for the island of Walcheren on the twenty-eighth and twenty-ninth of July.

The flank companies of the second battalion of the Coldstream embarked at Chatham, proceeded to the Nore, and were put on board ships of war.

★★★★★★

Return of the Grenadier and Light Infantry companies of the Coldstream, forming part of the Grenadier and Light Infantry battalions on service at Walcheren:—

The five companies forming the Grenadier battalion, commanded by Lieut.-Colonel P. Cocks, consisted of 5 captains and lieut.-colonels, 1 lieutenant and major, 14 lieutenants and captains, 1 adjutant, 1 quartermaster, 1 surgeon, 1 assistant-surgeon, 34 sergeants, 34 corporals, 19 drummers, 542 private men.

Officers of the Coldstream.

Lieut.-Colonel George Smyth.
Captain Thomas Thoroton.
    "   Hon, W. G. Crofton.
    "   H. W. Vachell.
 Quartermaster B. Selway.

Strength of the Grenadier company of the Coldstream;—
6 sergeants, 4 drummers, and 120 rank and file.

Headquarters, Fort de Batz, 24th Aug., 1809

The five companies forming the Light Infantry battalion, commanded by Lieut.-Colonel John Lambert, consisted of 5 captains and lieut.-colonels, 13 lieutenants and captains, 1 adjutant, 1 quartermaster, 1 surgeon, 1 assistant-surgeon, 35 sergeants, 35 corporals, 10 buglers, 545 private men.

Officers of the Coldstream.

Lieut.-Colonel Thomas Braddyll.

Captain Thomas Barrow.

   "   Newton Dickenson.

   "   Lord Alvanley.

Assistant-Surgeon John Crake.

Strength of the Light Infantry company of the Coldstream:—7 sergeants, 2 buglers, and 121 rank and file,

Headquarters, Ryland, 24th, Aug., 1809.

★★★★★★

The troops landed on the first of August, and invested Flushing. After a bombardment by sea and land, from which the town suffered greatly, General Monnet the governor demanded a suspension of hostilities, which terminated in the surrender of the town: the garrison, amounting to nearly six thousand men, were made prisoners of war. (The *London Gazette* of Tuesday, August 22nd, states that the garrison of Flushing amounted to 200 officers, 4085 rank and file, and 618 sick.) The force opposed to the British on the island rather exceeded nine thousand men.

Lord Chatham, whose army, long detained among unwholesome marches, began to suffer severely from fever, having ascertained that the enemy had availed themselves of the slowness of his proceedings to improve their means of defence, relinquished his intention of attacking Antwerp, and the greater part of the troops in consequence re-embarked on the fourteenth of September for England.

When Cromwell had achieved one of his greatest victories, he called it his "crowning mercy." The attempt against Antwerp, better known as the Walcheren expedition from having got no further, may be termed by England her "crowning absurdity," whether the magnitude and expense of the preparations are considered, or the original conception of the plan those splendid preparations were expected to realise.

All former disastrous and ill-considered debarkations on the enemy's coast are thrown into shade when compared with this memorable scheme for surprising an important fortress belonging to the most powerful monarch and most active warrior of the period; care being first taken to give him due notice of the approaching surprise by the preparatory siege of Flushing.

After lingering for weeks together in the pestilent islands of the Scheld, the English general, to his apparent astonishment discovered that Napoleon, whose resources and energy were known to the whole world, had contrived in the interval to render a *coup-de-main* on Antwerp altogether impracticable.

Much has been said of the inefficiency of the British commander on that occasion; and it was strongly urged by the opponents of the then existing administration, that an officer should not have been selected whose habitual dilatoriness had previously acquired for him the appellation of "the late" Lord Chatham.

But as his inglorious return was not attended with any personal consequences, there is reason to suppose that the fault rested elsewhere, and that the general's course had been marked out for him before he left England.

Tardiness of movement is at all times a very questionable evidence of military talent; but in the case of a *coup-de-main*, the application of the maxim "slow and sure" can only mean, sure not to succeed. The sufferings of the troops, and the cost to the country of twenty millions sterling, are yet remembered with indignant sorrow: it is to be hoped that future British Cabinets will at length learn from so many repeated lessons, that although such enterprises may succeed against detached islands cut off from all assistance, they cannot with prudence be adventured on the Continent with the inadequate force that a maritime power can suddenly and secretly convey on ship-board to the territories of a powerful enemy, whose troops may in a few hours be collected from every quarter in overwhelming numbers.

Although Napoleon had carried with him to the open field his strongest and most disciplined soldiers, it was pure infatuation to suppose that he had not left in France thousands who were fully competent for garrison duty; or that, having left them, they should be so placed as not to be within reach of his most important fortresses. Nothing happened which might not have been foretold, except the wonderment of the English ministers on finding that failure is the attendant of folly. Walcheren was retained till the twenty-third of December, when it was evacuated.

A battle was fought by the Spaniards on the nineteenth of November at Ocana, where their best troops were destroyed. (By the French account four thousand men were killed, twenty-six thousand taken prisoners, the remainder dispersed. The French admit their loss to have been one thousand seven hundred.) Napoleon considered this victory as the conclusion of the war, and exultingly exclaimed, in his speech to the Senate:

> I shall show myself beyond the Pyrenees, when the frightened leopard will fly to the sea to avoid shame, defeat, and death: my Imperial Eagles shall be planted on the ramparts of Cadiz, and be seen on the towers of Lisbon.

In this state of affairs Sir Arthur Wellesley, created Viscount Wellington, deemed it expedient to confine himself to the defence of Portugal: the army in consequence crossed the Tagus,

The brigade of Guards marched through Portalegre, Abrantes, Coimbra, and arrived at Vizeu on the thirtieth of December, where they were stationed. This place was also fixed on as the headquarters.

General Hill's corps was placed in and about Abrantes. The remainder of the army occupied Guarda, Celerico, Pinhel, and places in the neighbourhood. The River Cea ran along the front of the line.

The confident expectation expressed by the Emperor of France at this period, that "the leopard would fly to the sea," was not the result of a too sanguine temperament fondly bent on giving reality to its own unfounded wishes; the anticipation was that of a skilful soldier, founding his calculations on the ordinary rules of military science, and allowing his adversary, whose future movements he sought to divine, a fair portion of courage and talent.

The Spanish Army was annihilated; the spirit of that people appeared crushed; and no adequate force remained in Spain to impede the successful progress of the emperor's legions. Wellington, outnumbered by the French, retired through Portugal, a country deemed indefensible against the power of Napoleon. Everything seemed to indicate that the Peninsula would become the prey of the invader, and that the British were making for Lisbon to repeat the embarkation of Corunna: but the mind of their general rose above the difficulties of his situation; the leopard did not fly to the sea; he only drew back and took a more deadly spring.

Return of the officers of the 1st battalion Coldstream that embarked 31st of December, 1808, for the Peninsula.

Comps.	Captains.	Lieutenants.	Ensigns.
Gren.	Lt.-Col. John Ross	Capt. L. F. Adams ,, C. M. Christie ,, E. Jenkinson	
	,, ,, Rich. Hulse commanding the Bat.	,, Thos. Wood	Lord Kilcoursie E. N. Long
	,, ,, H. Mac Kinnon acting Major	¹ ,, R. Beckett	John Boswell Hon. J. Ashburnham
	Col. W. M. Peacocke	,, Hon. G. Pelham	Thomas Steele P. Sandilands
	¹ Brig.-Gen. W. P. Acland	,, Sir H. Sullivan	George Bowles Hon. F. H. Drummond
	Lt.-Col. T. Stibbert	,, F. M. Sutton	Thos. Sowerby John Prince
	,, Sir. W. Sheridan	¹ ,, H. F. Bouverie	E. Harvey Harry Parker
	,, Hon. H. Brand	¹ ,, H. F. Cooke	W. L. Walton
	,, ,, Js. Philips	,, F. M. Milman	W. Burroughs ¹ E. Lascelles
Light Inf.	,, ,, Jos. Fuller	,, G. Collier ,, W. H. Raikes ,, D. Mac Kinnon	

Adjutant, Captain Geo. Bryan.
Quarter-Master, John Holmes.
Battalion Surgeon, Charles Coombe.
Assistant-Surgeon, Thos. Rose.
,, ,, Wm. Whymper.
¹ On the Staff.

The following changes had taken place in December, 1809.

Joined.

Capt. Gore, Lt. James V. Harvey, Ensigns Lockwood, Hon. John Wingfield, Mildmay, Wedderburn, and White, Ensign Freemantle, Acting Adjutant 1st battalion.

Absent.

Col. Peacocke, Commandant at Lisbon, Brig.-Gen. Acland, Staff, Lieut.-Col. Sir W. Sheridan, Capt. F. M. Milman, and Assistant-Surgeon Whymper, prisoners of war. Capt. C. M. Christie, from prisoner of war, to 2d bat. in England. Capt. Thos. Steele, Capt. Harvey, and Capt. Burroughs, to 2d bat. at home on promotion. Ensign E. N. Long, drowned 9 March, Ensign Sandilands, from prisoner of war and sick to England. Ensign Freemantle, Adjutant to 2d bat. at home, Lt.-Col. J. Ross, Capt. R. Beckett, and Ensign H. Parker, killed July, 1809. Capt. E. Jenkinson, and Capt. and Adjutant Bryan, died of their wounds. Ensign Hon. John Ashburnham, supposed to be lost on passage home in Dec.

CHAPTER 7

Battle of Busaco

On the thirteenth of January the following letter appeared in Brigade Orders, directed to Colonel the Honourable Edward Stopford:

Vizeu, 13 January, 1810.

Sir,

I have taken frequent occasions of stating publicly the great satisfaction which the conduct of the Guards has invariably given me; which satisfaction has been renewed on the recent march through Portugal; in which, as they were the head of the column, they set the example to the other troops, of the most orderly and regular behaviour, I am anxious to testify this satisfaction in a manner which shall prove to them that the attention which they pay to their duty is not unobserved by their superiors; and if the commanding officers of the two battalions will be so kind as to recommend a sergeant each, I will recommend them to vacant ensigncies in the army.

(Signed)   Wellington.

Hon[ble] Col. Stopford.

Commanding 2nd Brigade of Guards.

Soult, with little opposition, forced the passes of the Sierra Morena, on the twentieth of January, which had been fortified, overthrowing twenty thousand men intended for their defence, and advanced into Andalusia. On the twenty-first of January, he reached Baylen. Seven days after, Victor joined him before Seville, which place opened its gates on the thirty-first, and Joseph Buonaparte entered the city in triumph. In February, Mortier was sent into Estramadura, and Victor marched for Cadiz, which was unprepared for defence. Vanegos, the governor, was much disliked, and resigned. A *Junta* was then elected by ballot.

The Duke of Albuquerque, in opposition to the orders he had received to march on Cordova, hastened in this extremity with all speed to Cadiz, and by the rapidity of his march arrived just in time (Feb. 4th), to barricade the bridge of Zuozo in the Isla de Leon. The French were therefore disappointed in their expectations of entering the place.

Six companies of the First Guards, two companies of the second battalion of the Coldstream, commanded by Lieutenant-Colonel Jackson, and three from the Third Guards under Brigadier-General Dilkes, marched from London to embark at Portsmouth for Cadiz, from whence they proceeded to the Isle of Leon.

In April, a force of between five and six thousand British and Portuguese was there collected under Lieutenant-General Graham. Both sides exerted themselves in constructing fortifications. The French strengthened Rota, Puerto Real, Puerto Santa Maria, and Chiclona. They formed entrenched camps between these places and at Trocadero; and established batteries, whence they threw enormous shells half filled with lead into the town. The English restored the old works and erected new ones along the Santa Petri River; they also cut a canal across the isthmus, near the Corta Dura, between the Isla and Cadiz. The Allies were considerably augmented. Strong reinforcements also arrived for the French in Spain, who had upwards of three hundred thousand men in different units of the Peninsula.

Towards the end of April, Lord Wellington moved from Vizeu to Celerico, at which place the brigade of Guards was quartered. (The Coldstream marched on the twenty-seventh, and reached Celerico next day. Part of the regiment quartered in the neighbouring villages.)

For some time, a powerful army had been assembling, which consisted of the Second, Sixth, and Eighth corps, under Marshal Massena. This was denominated "the Army of Portugal." Almeida was strengthened, in May, and hopes were entertained that it would detain the enemy some time, should Ciudad Rodrigo fall.

Massena commenced the siege of Ciudad Rodrigo in June, but the garrison did not capitulate till the tenth of July, after a siege of twenty-five days with open trenches. This general addressed a proclamation from Ciudad Rodrigo, in which he stated that the Emperor of the French had put under his orders an army of one hundred thousand men, to take possession of Portugal, and to expel the English, the pretended friends of the Portuguese, whose purposes were insidious

Return of two companies of the Second battalion of the Coldstream, at Isla de Leon, Tarifa, &c., from March 1810, to May 1811.

	Capt. and Lt.-Col.	Lts. and Capts.	Ensigns.	Quarter Master.	Assist. Surg.	Serjeants.	Drumrs.	Rank and File.	Total.
Consisting of . .	1	3	4	1	1	12	3	224	249
Joined from England 1st and 8th April, 1811 . }	.	.	.	.	1	1	.	42	44

		Present.		
		From	To	
Cap⁸ and Lt C¹ }	R. D. Jackson	Mar. 1810	March, 1811	{ Appointed Assist.-Quar.-Mast. Gen. in Portugal in March, 1811.
Lt.& Cap⁸ }	J. Hamilton	,, ,,	Remained on Staff	{ Appointed Deputy-Assist.-Quar.-Mast. Gen., Isla de Leon, in April, 1810
,,	W.C.Wynyard	Nov. ,,	Ditto	{ Joined and appointed Brig.-Major to Maj.-Gen. Dilkes in Nov. 1810. Do. to Col. Coote in May, 1811, and Dep.-Assist.-Adj-General in July, 1811, Isla de Leon.
,,	Hon. J.Walpole }	March ,,	May, 1811	{ In command of Lt.-Col. Woodford's Company. On leave from Oct. 1810 to Jan. 1811. Left the Station 24th May, and joined the 1st Battalion.
,,	M. Fortescue	,, ,,	23 June, 1810	{ " Leave to proceed to England, 23rd June, retiring from the Service."
Ens.	G. H. M. Greville }	,, ,,	May, 1811	{ Left the Station 24th May, and joined the 1st Batt.
,,	M. Watts	,, ,,	5 March	Killed at Barrosa, 5th March.
,,	C. A.F. Bentinck }	,, ,,	April	{ Wounded at do. Leave to England.
,,	John Talbot	,, ,,	May	{ Wounded at Barrosa, 5th March. Embarked with the detachment for England.
As⁸. Sur. }	C. Herbert	,, ,,	Oct. 1810	{ Leave to England in Oct. : retired from the Service.
,,	W. Whymper	April, 1811	May, 1811	{ Joined from England 1st April, 1811, and embarked for England on 4th May.
Qu⁸. M⁸. }	Serj. B. Selway (acts) }	Mar. 1810	,, ,,	{ Embarked with the detachment for England on 4 May.

	Lieut. and Captain.	Ensigns.	Staff.	Serjeants.	Drumrs.	Rank and File.
Left the Station at Isla de Leon, 4th and 24th May, 1811 . . .	1	2	2	12	3	243
Embarked for England 4th May .	.	1	2	9	3	145
Joined the 1st Battalion at camp near St. Olaia, 25th June . . .	1	1	.	3	.	98

Alex. Woodford promoted to Captain and Lieut.-Col. to one of these Companies, dated 8th March, 1810; "on the Staff in Sicily" to May, and "doing duty in London" from June, 1810.

and selfish: he added, that in opposing the emperor they opposed their true friend, who was governed by principles of universal philanthropy; that the English had put arms into their hands which would prove instruments of annihilation to them.

★★★★★★

British, Spanish, and Portuguese Armies:

With Lord Wellington, thirty thousand; with Lieutenant-General Hill, fourteen thousand; Reserve with Major-General Leith, ten thousand. There was also in co-operation a corps of Portuguese militia consisting of ten thousand, besides ten thousand Spanish troops under Romana; making a total of seventy-four thousand.

French Army under Massena:

The infantry of the Second, Sixth, and Eighth corps, sixty-two thousand; the cavalry six thousand; artillery, &c. four thousand. Besides which he was afterwards joined by two divisions of the Ninth corps under Drouet, consisting of ten thousand, as well as the remainder of the corps under General Claparède, eight thousand. A corps of thirteen thousand, under Mortier, was in co-operation on the south of the Tagus; making a total of one hundred and three thousand.

★★★★★★

He asked:

Can the feeble army, of the British general expect to oppose the victorious legions of the emperor? Already a force is collected sufficient to overwhelm your country. Snatch the moment that mercy and generosity offer! As friends you may respect us, and be respected in return; as foes you must dread us, and in the conflict must be subdued. The choice is your own, either to

85

meet the horrors of a bloody war, and see your country desolated, your villages in flames, your cities plundered; or to accept an honourable peace, which will obtain for you blessings that a vain resistance would deprive you of forever.

Ney with his corps attacked General Craufurd on the morning of the twenty-fourth, who was obliged to retreat behind the Coa; Craufurd, however, succeeded in maintaining the bridge till evening, notwithstanding the repeated attempts made by the enemy with a very superior force.

Previous to the investment of Almeida, Wellington took the precaution to withdraw his troops from Pinhel and Trancoso to the valley of the Mondego, behind Celerico, that he might retire leisurely if Massena advanced without waiting the surrender of that fortress. Almeida was invested by Massena: the batteries of the besiegers were not opened till towards the end of August, but the town unexpectedly surrendered on the twenty-seventh, owing to the explosion of the magazines in the citadel, by which calamity a great number of inhabitants and houses were destroyed.

On the fourth the following proclamation was issued by Lord Wellington:

The Portuguese must now perceive that no other means remain to avoid the evils with which they are threatened, but a determined and vigorous resistance, and a firm resolution to obstruct as much as possible the advance of the enemy into the interior of the kingdom, by removing out of his reach everything that may contribute to his subsistence, or facilitate his progress. The army under my command will protect as large a portion of the country as is possible; but it is obvious that the people alone can deliver themselves by a vigorous resistance, and preserve their goods by removing them beyond the reach of the enemy.

The duties, therefore, that bind me to His Royal Highness the Prince Regent of Portugal, and to the Portuguese nation, oblige me to make use of the power and authority with which I am intrusted to compel the careless and indolent to make the necessary efforts to preserve themselves from the dangers which threaten them, and to save their country. I therefore make known and declare, that all magistrates, and persons in authority, who shall remain in the villages and towns, after having received orders from the military officers to remove from

BATTLE OF BUSACO
Sept. 29th. 1810.

British ▰ French ▱

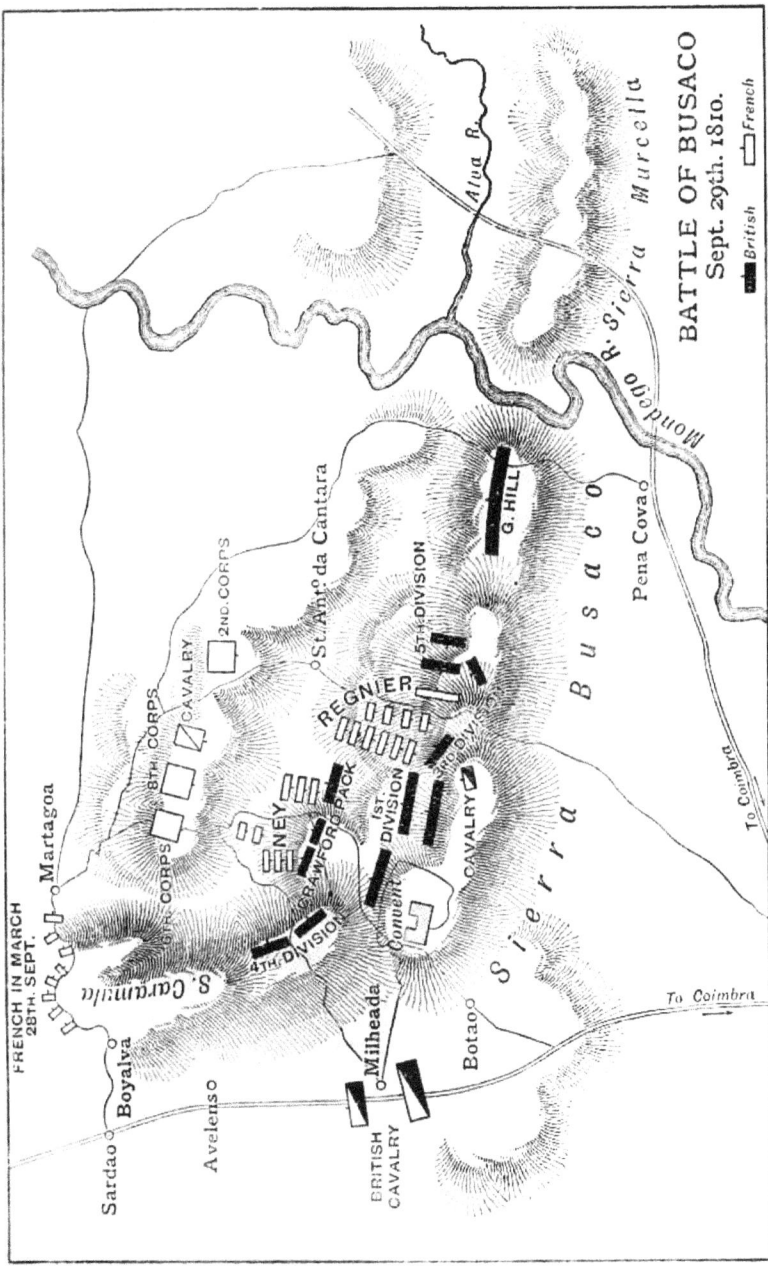

FRENCH IN MARCH
28TH. SEPT.

Sardao

Boyalva

Martagoa

S. Caramulla

Avelenso

Milheada

BRITISH CAVALRY

Botao

To Coimbra

8TH. CORPS

6TH. CORPS

CAVALRY

2ND. CORPS

St. Ant.o da Cantara

NEY

CRAWFORD PACK

4TH DIVISION

Convent

CAVALRY

REGNIER

1ST DIVISION

3RD. DIV.

5TH DIVISION

G. HILL

Sierra Busaco

Pena Covao

To Coimbra

Mondego R.

Alva R.

Sierra Murcella

R. Conch

them, and all persons, of whatsoever class they may be, who shall maintain the least communication with, or aid and assist the enemy in any manner, shall be considered as traitors to the state, and tried and punished in an offence so heinous requires.

Massena's army entered Portugal in three columns on September 16th, headed by Junot, Ney, and Regnier.

The Allies retreated in the finest order by the road on the left bank of the Mondego, leaving the other through Vizeu to Coimbra open.

The French Army concentrated at Vizeu; but their junction was retarded by a well-planned attack on September 20th made by Colonel Trant on a convoy of the enemy near Togal, within half a day's march of Vizeu. The colonel captured two officers and one hundred men, and caused the artillery under their convoy to fall back on Trancoso, which occasioned a delay of five days to the French general, as it obliged him to wait its arrival. (In an intercepted dispatch Massena says, "being obliged to wait five days at Vizeu for my artillery.")

By this occurrence Wellington gained time to execute one of the most brilliant manoeuvres of this brilliant campaign. At Ponte de Murcella, the day after Massena had reached Vizeu, the bridge was destroyed.

On the twenty-sixth Generals Hill and Leith joined the Allies, now in position on the heights of Busaco. The troops were ordered to conceal themselves as much as possible behind the brow of the hill. The French, placed immediately below, were distinctly seen from every part of the high ground, extending nearly eight miles from the Mondego in a northerly direction. A convent crowned the summit of Busaco, surrounded by extensive woods; this point was nearly three hundred feet high, but its elevation varied considerably in different places: two roads crossed the hill, one near the convent, the other more to the south. Sir Brent Spencer with the first division occupied the centre, on the right of which were the Guards; the Coldstream extended to Picton's division, which joined with Leith's; General Hill was on the extreme right; General Cole's division occupied the left. The light division was in advance, in front of the left and left centre. The cavalry under Sir Stapleton Cotton formed in the rear. General Fane's brigade was on the left of the Mondego.

Before day on the morning of the twenty-seventh, the British, who had been ordered on the previous evening to stand to their arms, were in readiness to receive the enemy. Ney's corps, formed in three masses, approached the convent; Junot was at some distance in the rear, and with him the greater part of the cavalry, Regnier attacked in two columns, and ascended a part of the hill, where he was opposed by the piquets and light troops of the third division, assisted by a flank fire of grape from some guns: notwithstanding this resistance he succeeded in gaining the summit in great force. The French had at first only to contend with the Eighty-Eighth regiment, belonging to part of Colonel Henry Mackinnon's brigade; but it was soon after reinforced by the Forty-Fifth and Eighth Portuguese regiments, also under his orders. The brigade thus united poured in a destructive fire of musketry, and furiously charged; in doing which they were joined by a brigade from Leith's division. They then drove the enemy with great impetuosity before them, who left upwards of seven hundred dead.

Marshal Ney was equally unsuccessful in his attack on the light division under Major-General Craufurd, who had judiciously formed behind the hill; so that on crowning the height, Ney's column had unexpectedly to encounter the effects of the artillery and musketry, followed by a charge. His column was not only routed, but the leading regiments were totally destroyed. The loss of the British and Portuguese did not much exceed twelve hundred; that of the French, on a moderate calculation, was supposed to be about five thousand.

Animated by the example of the British officers employed under Beresford in the organization of their army, and now associated with them in the field, the Portuguese, in many respects, did honour to the character recorded of them in the historical annals of that country.

Had Massena followed Ney's advice and attacked Busaco on the twenty-fifth, there would have been more chance of success, as it was at that time only partially occupied. On the twenty-seventh the issue of the attempt was at no time doubtful. His only alternative when he failed was to retire on Spain, or to turn the position, which he might equally have done on the preceding day. After the battle a Portuguese peasant was taken, and informed the enemy that the heights extending northwards from Busaco, called the Sierra de Carmula, were practicable for cavalry, and presented good roads to Coimbra and Oporto.

★★★★★★

Extract from Pampalona's *Aperçu Nouveau des Campagnes en Portugal*.

"*Le Général La Croix, en battant la campagne sur la droite de l'armée, ramassa un paysan qui lui indiqua la route de Boyalva à Sardao: il s'en approcha avec précaution, et hâta d'en instruire Massena, qui,*

*sur ce rapport, se décida à tourner la position de l'ennemi. C'est cette
circonstance qui fit dire au Maréchal Ney, que c'était la manoeuvre du
paysan; il ne qualifiait jamais cette manoeuvre autrement."*

★★★★★★

Massena then determined to turn the left of the Allied army.

Wellington intended that Colonel Trant's division of militia, consisting of about two thousand men, which from the commencement of the campaign had been employed in harassing the enemy's rear, should march to Sardao a few miles distant from Busaco. But as the order was conveyed through General Barcellar, who commanded in the north, that officer conceived that the movement was for the protection of Oporto, and with that belief sent Trant round by that city. After forced marches of two hundred miles, Trant at length reached Sardaoon the twenty-eighth, previous to the crossing of the Carmula by the French. His men, diminished by fatigue to about twelve hundred, were inadequate to resist an army headed by a numerous cavalry, marching in one column, especially as there were several passes, each of which required a more effective force than the armed peasantry under Trant to defend them.

Being informed on the thirtieth that the army had evacuated Busaco, Trant look post behind the Vouga. On his retreat he was charged by the enemy's cavalry and lost some men. Massena cleared the passes without difficulty during the twenty-eighth and twenty-ninth and marched for Coimbra, where he established his headquarters on the first of October. Leaving his hospital stores, and about five thousand sick and wounded under a guard, he advanced by Condexia, in expectation of falling in with the rear of Wellington's army, which during the night withdrew from the position and fell back to the south of the Mondego. The army then retired in the finest order towards their lines by the two parallel routes of Thomar and Lyria, occasionally halting to preserve the relative connexion of the two columns: that on the Thomar road was commanded by General Hill.

On the morning of the fifth of October Wellington continued his retreat, when the enemy advanced in great force, but were kept in check, with a trifling loss, which enabled the Allies to retire leisurely, the right by Thomar and Santarem, the centre through Batalha and Rio Mayor, and the left by Alcobaça and Obidos. The weather at this time was cold, and the rain fell in torrents. Massena continued to follow by the Rio Mayor road, and in the afternoon of the tenth drove the Allies out of the village of Sobral. On same day, October 10th, the British troops were concentrated within their lines. Lord Wellington's foresight in the formation of these extensive works was worthy of his fame and extraordinary talents; they were begun and completed without attracting any particular notice. The British troops were as much surprised at finding themselves in their strongly-fortified and impregnable position, as the French commander was astonished and confounded when he saw that the further progress of his overwhelming force was effectually arrested. Next day six thousand Spaniards, under the Marquis de la Romana, joined Wellington from the Alentejo.

The lines of Torres Vedras extended from the Tagus on the right, or east, to the sea on the west. In November, General Hill's division occupied the village of Alhandra on the right, which was flanked by a number of gunboats; Craufurd's division joined their left. On the mountain which overhung Sobral, and completely commanded the great road to Lisbon, was a strong redoubt, occupied by a brigade of Portuguese commanded by General Pack. The first division under Lieutenant-General Spencer, including the brigade of Guards, was stationed in the centre. Picton's division communicated with Spencer's on the right, and with General Cole's on the left, which last carried on the line of defence to the sea.

Whilst affairs were in this state south of the Mondego, Trant, having taken up a position on the Vouga to cover Oporto after the retreat of the armies from Busaco, had resolved to surprise whatever force Massena might have left in Coimbra, and accordingly reached Mealhada in the night of the sixth of October, From thence he advanced next day to Coimbra, in front of which, at the village of Fernos, he came suddenly on one of the enemy's advanced posts. He entered the gates unobserved, and after an hour's resistance the French, to the number of five thousand, chiefly sick and wounded, surrendered. Trant's loss did not exceed twenty-five or thirty men, A company of the Imperial Marine Guards fell into his hands, with the hospital stoics and medical staff of the enemy. By this movement of Trant's, Massena was left to the scanty resources of his immediate vicinity, being deprived from that time of all communication beyond his own pat roles in the direction of the Rivers Zezere and Mondego.

The French Army suffered greatly from want of supplies and exposure to the weather. Marshal Massena, who could no longer conceal from himself the hopelessness of the task he had undertaken, after remaining inactive upwards of a month, retreated on the night of the fourteenth of November, for the purpose of taking up a line of cantonments in the vicinity of Thomar.

The Allied Army followed the enemy towards Santarem, when the Guards passed through Alenquer and Cartaxo. Wellington made a demonstration for an attack. The Guards were to cross the causeway; but the guns not arriving, the advance was postponed until the following day. At six o'clock a.m. on the twentieth the brigade of Guards assembled at their alarm-post; but in consequence of the rain that had fallen during the night, the low country in front of the enemy's position was so flooded as to render any attempt at passing dangerous and uncertain.

On the enemy being discovered in great force, the troops were withdrawn, and the army went into cantonments. The Guards returned to Cartaxo, at which place headquarters were established: the remainder of the army were cantoned at Alcoentre, Rio Mayor, Azembuja, Alenquer, and Villa Franca. Hill's corps crossed the Tagus, and went into quarters at Barcos, Chamusca, and Caregiro.

At the end of December General Drouet with ten thousand men reinforced Massena's army: this corps went into cantonments in and about Lyria.

RETURN OF OFFICERS OF THE FIRST BATTALION OF THE COLDSTREAM FOR THE YEAR 1810.

	Officers present in the Peninsula.	From	To		Officers absent.	Cause of absence.	From	To
Col.	Richard Hulse	1 Jan.	Nov.	Lt.-G.	John Calcraft (1st Major)	Leave	1 Jan.	31 Dec.
..	H. Mac Kinnon	,,	Feb.	Col.	Richard Hulse	Commanding a Brigade	Dec.	,,
Lt.-C.	Joseph Fuller	,,	June	Col.	H. Mac Kinnon	Commanding a Brigade	March	,,
,,	Thomas Stibbert	,,	31 May		W. M. Peacocke	Commandant at Lisbon	1 Jan.	,,
,,	Hon. H. Brand	,,	31 Dec.	Br.-G.	Wroth P. Acland	Staff at home	,,	,,
,,	James Philips	,,	,,	Lt.-C.	Joseph Fuller	Posted to 2d Batts.	June	,,
,,	Sir G. Stirling, Bart.	Feb.	,,	,,	M. Lord Aylmer	Asst. Adjt. Genl.	1 Jan.	,,
,,	George Smyth	Oct.	,,	,,	Thomas Stibbert	Leave to England. Retired	1 June	27 June
Capt.	E. Dalling (Major)	Feb.	,,	,,	Sir W. Sheridan	Prisoner of war	1 Jan.	31 Dec.
,,	Lucius F. Adams	1 Jan.	,,	Capt.	H. F. Bouverie	Staff (Acting Mily. Secy.)	,,	—
,,	George Collier	,,	,,	,,	Henry F. Cooke	Staff (Deputy Asst. Adjutant General)	,,	31 Dec.
,,	Sir H. Sullivan, Bart.	,,	,,	,,	John Hamilton	Depy. Assistant Qur. Master Genl. Cadiz	April	,,
,,	Francis Sutton	,,	23 Nov.	,,	Francis Sutton	Sick leave to Engd.	24 Nov.	,,
,,	W. H. Raikes	,,	31 Dec.	,,	F. M. Milman	Prisoner of war	1 Jan.	,,
,,	Thomas Gore	,,	24 Oct.	,,	Thomas Gore	Sick leave to Engd.	25 Oct.	,,
,,	H. W. Vachell	Feb.	31 Dec.	,,	Thomas Wood	Leave to Engd. on resignation	29 Nov.	,,
,,	Thomas Wood	1 Jan.	28 Nov.	,,	Hon. G. Pelham	A. D. C. to Br. Genl. Campbell.	1 Jan.	—
,,	Thomas Barrow	Sept.	31 Dec.	,,	Hon. W. G. Crofton	On his way to join	Dec.	—
,,	D. Mac Kinnon	1 Jan.		,,	Henry Dawkins	Brigr. Major to Hon. E. Stopford	June	31 Dec.
Ens.	George Bowles	,,	Feb.	,,	Thomas Steele	On his way to join	Dec.	,,
,,	John Boswell	,,	March	,,	George Bowles	Promd. in 2d Batt.	Feb.	,,
,,	Hon. Francis Drummond	,,	22 July	,,	John Boswell	Ditto.	March	—
,,	Thomas Sowerby	,,	7 Sept.	,,	Hon. F. Drummond	Ditto.	23 July	,,
,,	E. Lascelles	,,	,,	,,	Thomas Sowerby	Ditto.	8 Sept.	,,
,,	John Prince	,,	April	,,	Edwd. Lascelles	Ditto.	,, ,,	,,
,,	G. F. A. Lord Kilcoursie	,,	11 Sept.	,,	P. Sandilands	Sick in England	1 Jan.	,,
,,	J. V. Harvey, (Lieut.)	,,	31 Dec.	Ens.	John Prince	Ditto. Posted to 2d Batts.	April	,,
,,	W. L. Walton	,,	,,	,,	Lord Kilcoursie	Leave to England	12 Sept.	,,
,,	W. Lockwood	,,	,,	,,	Hon. J. Ashburnham	Supposed to be drowned on passage to England	Jan.	—
,,	Hon. John Wingfield	,,	,,	,,	G. H. Percival	Sick in England	,,	Sept.
,,	Paulet St. John Mildmay	,,	,,			Taken prisoner 6 Aug. 1809: Made his escape 20 Dec. 1809.	1 Jan.	25 Feb.
,,	A. Wedderburn	,,	,,	Ast. Sur. }	W. Whymper			
,,	Charles White	,,	,,			Sick leave to England	10 Nov.	31 Dec.
,,	Thomas Bligh	Feb.	,,	Ens.	John Mills	On his way to join	Dec.	,,
,,	Charles Shawe	,,	,,					
,,	G. H. Percival	Oct.	,,					
,,	William Stothert	,,	,,					
,,	W. G. Baynes	Sept.	,,					
,,	John S. Cowell	Oct.	,,					
Adjut.	H. Dawkins (Capt.)	Feb.	June					
,,	J. Freemantle (Capt.)	Oct.	31 Dec.					
Q.-Mr.	John Holmes	1 Jan.	,,					
Surgn.	Charles Coombe	,,	,,					
Ast. Sur. }	Thomas Rose	,,	,,					
,,	W. Whymper	26 Feb.	9 Nov.					

CHAPTER 8

Barrosa, Fuentes d'Honor & Albuera

Seven thousand men for the army under Wellington arrived in the Tagus on the fourth of March, 1811.

The following General Order was issued at Cartaxo:

Adjutant-General's Office, Cartaxo, 4 March, 1811.
General Order:

1. As the object in assembling the troops in any station to witness a punishment is to deter others from the commission of the crime for which the criminal is about to suffer, the Commander of the Forces requests that upon every occasion on which the troops are assembled for this purpose, the order may be distinctly read and explained to them, and that every man may understand the reason for which the punishment in to be inflicted.

2. As during the two years, during which the brigade of Guards have been under the command of the Commander of the Forces, not only no soldier has been brought to trial before a general court-martial, but no one has been confined in a public guard, the Commander of the Forces desires, that the attendance of this brigade at the execution tomorrow may be dispensed with.

On the night of the fifth the French retreated, and headquarters removed to Santarem, where the Guards were stationed.

General Houghton's brigade crossed the Tagus, on the 6th. The light division, followed by the rest of the army, advanced; on their approach the enemy retired from Thomar, concentrated at Pombal. The Allied Army came up with them on the evening of the eleventh, too late, however, for a general attack: the day closed with a smart skirmish, when the enemy were so vigorously driven out of the town that they had not time to blow up the bridge which had been previously mined. Massena retreated in the night; but before quitting Pombal he set it on fire.

Ney was found posted with a strong force in front of Redinha; the masses deployed, and the British moved in three lines across the plain; the enemy's rear-guard, after an obstinate resistance, hastily retired on Condeixa.

On this occasion the loss was nearly equal, not exceeding altogether four hundred men.

Massena's object was to retard the advance of the Allies, and in this he succeeded, as the positions on which his rear was generally posted required a march of several hours to turn their flank.

General Montbrun with a force of cavalry and a few guns summoned Coimbra. The place was saved by the firm reply and admirable conduct of Trant, although he had only two hundred of his militia with him, having received orders from General Barcellar on the eleventh instant to withdraw the greater part of his force to cover Oporto. The French general, under the impression that a British attachment had landed at Figuiera to reinforce that officer, then gave up all idea of crossing the Mondego.

The enemy occupied strong ground at Condeixa, and appeared determined to continue stationary; but this short halt was only intended by Massena to give time for his baggage to precede him on the Ponte de Marcella road. This being ascertained by Lord Wellington, he resolved to frustrate the plan, and instantly despatched Picton's division, with orders to make a circuit of some miles, and turn the enemy's left. About three o'clock Picton was discovered by the French rearguard, and his appearance occasioned great confusion among them.

The enemy fired the town, and their columns fell back on Cazal Nova, at which place Ney halted in so formidable a position that it was again found necessary to turn his flank: on this being done, he fell back on another In short, the country presented a succession of favourable positions adapted to check pursuit, by which the French rear-guard was enabled to retire in good order, March 14th, on Miranda de Corvo. From this place Wellington once more obliged the enemy to retreat, which caused them to destroy the greater part of their stores, ammunition, and baggage, as they were deficient in the means of transport.

Next day the Allies were detained several hours by a thick fog, which cleared about nine, when the troops continued the pursuit of

C. Ortega
C. Penas
Santander
Corunna
Ferrol
Oviedo
Valmaseda
Minho
Lugo
Espinosa
Leon
R. Esla
Villafranca
Saldana
Astorga
Vigo
R. Sil
Carrion
Benevente
Valdaras
Villapando
Valladolid
Medina
Oporto
R. Douro
Tordessilas
Salamanca
Almeida
Ciudad Rodrigo
Villacastian
Busaco
Fuentes de Onoro
Guadarama
40°
Coimbra
Aranjuez
Talavera
Vimieiro
Abrantes
Toledo
Tagus R.
Santarem
Torres Vedras
S P A
LISBON
Badajos
Medellin
Alburea
PORTUGAL
Sierra
Guadiana R.
Baylen
Curdova
Guadalquivir R.
Seville
C. St. Vincent
Malaga
Cadiz
Barrosa
36°
C. Trafalgar
Gibraltar
8°
4°

Map of the
SPANISH CAMPAIGN.

English Miles

0 20 40 60 80 100   200

the French through Miranda de Corvo. This place having been burnt, was a heap of smoking ruins.

Ney was strongly posted in the afternoon of the fifteenth with his right on a wood, and his left resting on the village of Foz d'Aronse. A false attack was made on his right; at the same moment his left was surprised by Picton, and an advantageous position being selected for the horse artillery, the French were thrown into disorder, which was increased by the darkness that so soon follows sunset in Portugal. Numbers of the enemy were trampled to death. In their confusion they also fired on each other; and the bridge was so crowded from their anxiety to cross the river, that no less than two hundred and fifty were drowned.

At half-past seven o'clock next morning the Coldstream advanced from the low ground to crown the height previously occupied by General Picton's division.

After halting a day to enable the commissariat to forward supplies, of which the Allied troops were in great want, the light division forded the Ceira on the seventeenth of March, and the remainder of the army crossed over a bridge constructed during the night. The enemy stationed themselves behind the Alva, having destroyed the bridge near Pombeira and Marcella. Wellington ordered two divisions to ford the river near Pombeira, which movement threatened to cut off the enemy's communication with Celerico, and compelled Massena to retire in great haste, on the eighteenth, leaving the foragers he had sent out to their fate: nearly a thousand of them were taken. And here the French again destroyed their baggage and ammunition.

About one o'clock p.m. on the nineteenth, the Guards left the heights above Pombeira; the first division forded the Alba at Sarsedas.

From the deficiency of supplies Wellington found it impossible to proceed; he was therefore obliged to wait for the arrival of provisions, and in consequence Massena on the twenty-first reached Celerico unmolested.

The army having halted a lew days, marched on Celerico, where the brigade of Guards arrived on the twenty-ninth.

Massena occupied Guarda, a town built on the top of a steep hill, forming part of the Estrella range of mountains: the place commanded from its position the whole surrounding country. Thus situated, he conceived himself secure from any attack, Wellington, nevertheless, determined to make the attempt. His arrangements were so skilful, that on the morning of the twenty-ninth the Allied columns were not discerned by the enemy until they had nearly gained the summit; the French, surprised and confounded, retreated without firing a shot, from perhaps the strongest ground they could have occupied.

Massena, however, still felt anxious to make it appear that he could maintain himself in Portugal, for this purpose he took a position along the Coa; his right, extending to Ruivina, protected the ford of Rapoulha de Coa; his left reached to Sabugal, and a corps was stationed at Alfayates.

Trant and Wilson had crossed the Coa near Almeida to threaten the enemy's communication with Spain. The right of the Allies was opposite Sabugal, the left at the bridge of Ferreras. At daybreak on the third of April the cavalry forded the Coa on the right. The light division passed three miles above Sabugal; the fifth was to cross the bridge; and the third division forded at a short distance above. The bridge of Ferreras was observed by the seventh division, and the sixth was stationed opposite Ruivina. The morning was dark, with thick fog accompanied by storms of rain.

The action was commenced by a battalion of the Rifle brigade, who after being charged, got possession of an enclosure, which they retained against the efforts of the whole of Regnier's corps until the remainder of the light division came to their assistance. The contest was then carried on with great vigour; but on the approach of the fifth division, the French retired on Rendo, leaving three hundred dead, and a howitzer on the field, besides twelve hundred prisoners. The loss of the Allies did not exceed one hundred and seventy killed and wounded. (The French had intended to fire a *feu-de-joie* for the birth of the King of Rome.) The pursuit continued to Alfayates, when the French entered Spain. Portugal, with the exception of the garrison of Almeida, was now entirely freed from their troops.

Thus, ended the third French invasion of Portugal under Massena, "*l'enfant gâté de la Fortune.*" Napoleon had sent with him to that devoted country the chosen veterans of France; men who had conquered at Marengo, at Austerlitz, and Jena. At first the French Army imagined the lines of Torres Vedras might be easily forced, and considered the entire subjugation of Portugal, the plunder of Lisbon, and the favourite idea of sending the British to their ships, objects of easy accomplishment. Such were the "*Châteaux en Espagne*" built by the French when this memorable invasion was undertaken; nor were their illusive hopes destroyed until they had approached those lines.

When, however, Massena found himself unable to make any impression on them, and that neither forage, provisions, nor any other necessary for an army, could be obtained, he, with bitter conviction, saw that the superior foresight and skill of Wellington had destroyed all his hopes of aggrandisement, of glory, of the crown of Portugal, and of additional trophies for the troops of Napoleon !

It is impossible for an Englishman and a soldier not to exult in the recollection of this glorious campaign. But the writer forbears to enlarge on the subject: the facts speak for themselves, and the indignant reprimand which Massena received from Napoleon through his Minister-at-War, alike expressive of the surprise and disappointment of that excellent judge of military operations, is the proper commentary on the successful defence of Portugal under circumstances originally so unpromising.

In his address to the Portuguese, Massena had announced that he entered their country at the head of one hundred thousand men, and asked, with no small appearance of reason, whether the feeble army of the British general could reasonably expect to oppose the victorious legions of France? The marshal answered his own question when he was at length compelled to declare in his justification to his angry master, that the principles of military science did not permit him to attempt the lines of Torres Vedras.

It is no reproach to Sir John Moore, who ranked among the bravest and most intelligent British generals of his time, to say, that what all men but Wellington thought impossible, appeared impossible to him.

The letter of that general to Lord Castlereagh, written at no very long period before Sir Arthur Wellesley directed the lines of Torres Vedras to be constructed, will prove how far even Sir John Moore was from supposing it to be within the reach of human ability to check an enemy at Lisbon, and to baffle any attempt on that capital.

Salamanca, November 25, 1808.

I am not prepared at this moment to answer minutely Your Lordship's question respecting the defence of Portugal; but I can say generally that the frontier of Portugal is not defensible against a superior force. It is an open frontier—all equally rugged, but all equally to be penetrated. If the French succeed in Spain, it will be vain to attempt to resist them in Portugal. The Portuguese are without military force; and from the experience of their conduct under Sir Arthur Wellesley, no dependence is to be placed on any aid they can give.

The British must, in that event, I conceive, immediately take steps to evacuate the country. Lisbon is the port, and therefore the only place from whence the army with its stores can embark. Elvas and Almeida are the only fortresses on the frontier. The first is, I am told, a respectable work. Almeida is defective, and could not hold out ten days against a regular attack. I have ordered a depot of provisions for a short consumption to be formed there, in case this army should be obliged to fall back; perhaps the same should be done at Elvas. In this case we might check the progress of the enemy whilst the stores are embarking and arrangements are made for taking off the army. *Beyond this the defence of Lisbon or Portugal is not to be thought of.*

I have the honour to be, &c.

John Moore.

The French generals, to whom every inch of ground in the Peninsula was known, held the same opinion.

Napoleon, determined to bring the whole of the Peninsula under the sway of France, had formed the plan of placing his brother Joseph on the throne of Spain, and one of his generals, either Junot or Massena, on that of Portugal. The success which had hitherto attended the French arms, the ignorance of military affairs, and the want of every requisite for the formation of an army, either among the Spaniards or Portuguese, were such—the imbecility of their governments, the superstition, it may be added, the state of degradation into which the population of both countries had sunk, were so notorious, that neither the Emperor of the French, nor any of his marshals, imagined that serious opposition to his schemes would be attempted.

He boldly proclaimed to France and to Europe that he would plant his eagles on the towers of Lisbon! and when Napoleon uttered a prophecy, he had prepared what he deemed ample means for its accomplishment. No sooner did he find himself unexpectedly opposed in the Peninsula, than he became fully aware of the importance of carrying his point; not so much from the vanity of disposing of the thrones of two such kingdoms, as from the conviction, that if he failed in his attempt, the character he had acquired and wished to confirm, of invincibility, would be lost; and that the effect on France, his army, and Europe, would prove highly injurious to his hitherto admitted supremacy. He therefore poured his legions into Spain; determined by force, or, if necessary, by extermination, to obtain that which the good-will of the people would not grant.

The amount of the French troops in Spain and Portugal was nearly three hundred thousand men; and the only obstacle to the entire subjugation of the Peninsula was the force under Wellington, consisting of forty-eight thousand eight hundred and fifty-seven, (Adjutant-General's Returns, January, 1811. Out of which 9,298 were in hospital); not more than one-sixth of the number of the French.

★★★★★★

General state of the French army in the Peninsula. From the Imperial Muster-Rolls, January 15th, 1811.

KING JOSEPH Commanding.

Present under arms.		Detached.		Absent.	Effective.	Horses.	
Men.	Horses.	Men.	Horses.	Hospital.	Men.	Cavalry.	Draught.
295,227	52,462	17,780	4714	48,831	361,838	41,189	15,987

—From Col. Napier's Appendix

In 1810 the grand total of effective men in Spain amounted to 369,924 men, 43,574 horses, and 17,145 draught horses.—From Col. Napier's Appendix

★★★★★★

Napoleon's orders to his commanders were to expel the English; and indeed, the execution of these orders, after the retreat of Sir John Moore, was considered by the French generals by no means difficult.

Wellington, conscious that his handful of men would have to contend against the whole French power in the Peninsula, which sooner or later would be brought to bear against him; knowing also the little reliance that could be placed either on the Spanish *Junta* or on the Spanish generals who commanded their troops, conceived the idea of fortifying the passes in front of Lisbon; and with the Tagus on one flank, and the sea on the other, to make a stand, and there to decide whether the conquest of the Peninsula by Napoleon, or its liberation by himself, should be achieved. This plan was not a conception of the moment; it was deliberately adopted after the maturest calculation of practicability and attendant difficulties.

Wellington saw that Portugal might be defended by lines drawn so as to cover Lisbon, and secure to the protecting force supplies from the Tagus on one side and the sea on the other.

★★★★★★

The following is the substance of the Duke of Wellington's observations on the defence of Lisbon:

"The Tagus cannot be passed but at a certain point; you have therefore only to rest one flank of the army on that river, and, having a naval superiority you may defy any attack, and are perfectly secure on that side. The sea covers the other flank, the distance of which from the river is not more than twenty miles. An army therefore of forty or fifty thousand men may resist, in a mountainous and difficult country, any force which an enemy could bring into the field, even without entrenchments."

As the British Army consisted of a great proportion of militia and Portuguese troops, in whom at one time not much confidence could be placed, the duke thought it a necessary security to cause works to be erected; and, having plenty of time, they were prepared accordingly. Had the Allies been less ably commanded, those lines would never have been constructed, and the troops must have embarked, leaving Portugal to its fate.

★★★★★★

The successful result of his measures, and the ignorant declamations uttered against them in Parliament, are now matter of history.

At Torres Vedras the French met with a complete check; their plan of operations was entirely broken; and they were obliged to retreat, discomfited and disheartened, into Spain, whither they were followed by the British, flushed with the anticipation of success, and with confidence in their leader which was the pledge of victory.

The political influence of this retreat can scarcely be appreciated: it proved to Europe that the French were not invincible; it evinced the good effects of a determined opposition to the ambitious projects of Napoleon, and encouraged Russia in withstanding the outrageous demand, that British commerce should be excluded from her ports. The lines of Torres Vedras broke the wand of the enchanter, and led to that resistance by the Northern States of Europe, which ended in the downfall of French dominion, and of a man as remarkable for the great powers of his mind as for his inordinate ambition; whose activity and military talents were commensurate with his anxiety to extend his sway over mankind, and with his indifference to the evils he inflicted on his fellow-creatures in pursuing that object.

The desolation in Portugal occasioned by Massena's invading army can scarcely be conceived: not an article of subsistence (see *Moniteur*) was to be found; every town and village was deserted; the wine that could not be consumed was left running in the gutters; the corn-stacks burnt; in the houses, which from want of means or time were

103

not destroyed, all the furniture was broken; neither horse, mule, cow, nor ass, not even a goat, could be seen. The women captured by the French in their marauding excursions were brought in as to a market and sold for the benefit of the captors; many of these unfortunate females were left to perish by famine and disease remote from their native villages. Lord Wellington in his dispatch says:

> The conduct of the French Army, throughout this retreat, has been marked by a barbarity seldom equalled, and never surpassed. Even in the towns of Torres Novas, Thomar, and Pernes, in which headquarters of some of the corps had been for some months, and in which the inhabitants were induced by promises of good treatment to remain, they were plundered and many of their houses destroyed on the night the enemy withdrew from their position; and they have since burned every town and village through which they passed.

After the enemy quitted Portugal, in April, the Allies were stationed near the Duas Casas, the outposts at Gallegos and on the Agueda. All communication between the garrison of Almeida and the French was cut off.

The brigade of Guards halted on the ninth at Almadilla, having forded the Coa above Sabugal, and passing through Aldea Velha. On the seventeenth the Coldstream moved, for the convenience of quarters, to Puebla.

Badajoz had surrendered to Soult on the eleventh of March, when the garrison laid down their arms; and on the twenty-first of February ten thousand infantry and ten hundred cavalry had been embarked at Cadiz for Tarifa, to make a diversion by attacking the enemy's rear at Chiclana. The tempestuous state of the weather forced them into Algesiras, where they landed and marched the following day for Tarifa, There they were joined by the Twenty-Eighth regiment, the flank companies of the Ninth and Eighty-Second regiments, amounting to about four thousand five hundred men, including two companies of Portuguese and some German hussars, under General Graham.

On the twenty-seventh of February General La Pena with about seven thousand Spaniards arrived; and next day the troops were reorganised, and Graham, taking command of the British, consented to act under the Spanish general. The vanguard was given to Lardizabel, and the cavalry were commanded by Colonel Whittingham, Marescal del Campo in the service of Spain.

In the nights of the third and fourth of March the enemy attacked the Spanish force, and were repulsed. Next day a detachment from St. Roque joined the Allies under General Bejines, but retired after some skirmishing. La Pena then opened his communication with the Isla de Leon, and ordered his troops to crown the heights of Bermeja, having directed Graham to support him. The general obeyed; but no sooner had he entered the wood than the Spanish commander withdrew, giving orders that his cavalry should follow him. La Pena then marched to the River Santi Petri, leaving the heights of Barrosa, which were covered with baggage, to be protected by only five battalions and four guns.

During Graham's advance two divisions of the enemy were discovered; one of them made for the heights of Barrosa, the other marched on his flank.

The Duke of Belluno had under his command nine thousand men belonging to the divisions of Laval, Ruffin, and Villatte, with fourteen guns; about two thousand five hundred belonging to the division of the latter had orders to watch the Spaniards at the Santi Petri and Bermeja.

The ground was an extensive plain, nearly surrounded by a pine forest, and crossed by uneven sandy heights, which rose from the shore. The hill of Barrosa was about a mile from the mouth of the Santi Petri.

The French general perceiving Graham's situation. and aware of the relative position of the Spanish troops, immediately ordered Laval to attack him, whilst he attempted to cut off the detachment on the road to Medina; for which purpose he ascended the opposite side of the hill, where the five battalions, with the guns, baggage, &c. had been left by La Pena. The enemy succeeded in taking three of the guns; on which the Spanish troops immediately dispersed.

Graham, finding it impossible to retreat without giving his adversary a decided advantage, at once determined on becoming the assailant.

The British column had been marching, right in front, for an hour and a half through the woody when Major Brown told General Graham that the enemy were formed on a rising ground which the column had recently quitted. The troops in consequence countermarched under a heavy fire of artillery, and formed in two masses. The right column, led by Brigadier-General Dilkes, moved against Ruffin, who had crowned the summit of Barrosa: at the same time Colonel

BATTLE OF
BARROSA
5th March 1811.

A E JOHNSON 1828

Cavalry ▭ Allies Infantry ▭ French ▭ Artillery

SCALES
Military Scale 2½ Feet each

English Mile

Positions before and after the battle coloured light

Retreat
of the French

VERA CRUZ Co.

CERRO DEL
PUERCO

CERRO
CREEK
40,000

CERRO

VIGIA DE LA BARROSA

To Cadiz

To Barrosa

Laval's Division

British

Lieutenant Three crosses

Graham's Division

Two Spanish Regiments

Tower of the Gonzales
Casa de las Gonzales

French Camp

Bermeja

French Lines

Medina de Sidonia

French Post

Santi Petri

From Chiclana

RIO DE SANTI PETRI

Puente de Santi Petri

Puente de la de Santi Petri

Canal de Sti Petri

A T L A N T I C   O C E A N

Wheatly attacked the right of the enemy, and, after a sharp contested fire, continued to advance. The Eighty-Seventh regiment, and two companies of the Coldstream Guards under Lieutenant-Colonel Jackson, made an intrepid charge, which threw the enemy back in great disorder. Ruffin's troops on the hill manfully contested the height; but, notwithstanding all their efforts, the English drove the French from the position, on which they left three guns, after a severe loss.

General Graham was unable to follow up his success, as his men had been under arms for twenty-four hours, during which time they received no supply of rations.

The attack on Barrosa, which did not continue more than two hours, reflects great credit on the troops engaged.

The enemy suffered severely, and lost two generals, Ruffin and Rousseau, the latter being mortally wounded; one eagle, six guns, and upwards of two thousand five hundred men killed, wounded, and prisoners. The British loss amounted to eleven hundred and sixty-nine. The following is a copy of General Graham's dispatch:

> Where all have so distinguished themselves, it is scarcely possible to discriminate any as the most deserving of praise. Your Lordship will, however, observe how gloriously the brigade of Guards, under Brigadier-General Dilkes, with the commanders of battalions, Colonel Honourable C. Onslow and Lieutenant-Colonel Sebright, (wounded,) as well as the three separated companies under Colonel Jackson, maintained the high character of His Majesty's household troops.

The casualties of the detachment of the Coldstream Guards engaged were:—one ensign, eight rank and file killed; two ensigns, one sergeant, forty-five rank and file wounded. Killed, Ensign Watts; wounded, Ensigns Bentinck and Talbot.

Marshal Beresford, who was in the Alentejo, received orders early in March to invest Badajoz without delay, that the garrison might not have sufficient time allowed them to repair the damage done to the fortifications during the last siege.

Almeida was now closely blockaded; Massena had retired on Salamanca, for the purpose of restoring to his troops that confidence, order, and discipline, which they had lost in his hasty retreat. After this he advanced, having been considerably reinforced, and readied Ciudad Código on the twenty-fifth of April.

Wellington took advantage of the enemy's absence to visit the

BATTLE OF BARROSA

troops in the Alentejo under Beresford, and, having made all the necessary preparations in conjunction with him, returned to his headquarters at Villa Formosa on the twenty-eighth,

Massena on the second of May crossed the frontier with about forty thousand men and five thousand cavalry. The British were reduced to about thirty-two thousand infantry and twelve hundred cavalry.

At twelve o'clock the same day the Coldstream received orders to march by the left of Almadilla, where they remained till late in the evening. During the night the brigade of Guards moved to Nava d'Aver, and on the third the army was placed in position.

The River Coa runs in a northerly direction; its banks are very steep, and render the passage very difficult for an army, except at some few places, which are at the bridges of Almeida and Castello Bora, about seven miles above and at the ford of St. Roque, near Freynada. Almeida is situated on the right of the Coa; consequently, Wellington had no option but to engage with the river in his rear.

The British commander, on changing his position, found it necessary to extend it to the right, as in case of disaster the bridge of Sabugal was the only place where the army could cross the Coa; the right wing was therefore extended to Nava d'Aver, which was occupied by Julian Sanchez, and supported by the seventh division. Wellington took up his ground behind the river of Duas Casas: the first, third, and seventh divisions were strongly posted in rear of Fuentes d' Honor; the sixth and light divisions watched the bridge of Almeida across the Duas Casas: and the fifth division the fords across that river at Fort Conception and Aldea d'Obispo. Trant's and Wilson's militia had been in observation on Almeida, and were relieved by Pack's brigade on the sixteenth of April. The investment of Almeida was placed under the direction if General Alexander Campbell.

The enemy formed, on the third, behind the Duas Casas: their left overlooked the village of Fuentes; their right tended about two miles, running nearly in a parallel direction to the position of the Allies. The same afternoon the French resolutely attacked the village of Fuentes, where a most gallant resistance was made; fresh troops were constantly supplied by both parties: the contest continued till night, when the assailants were finally driven back across the Duas Casas.

The French marshal was occupied on the fourth in reconnoitring the position. During the night the Duke d'Abrantes' corps with the cavalry from Almeida moved to the left. About six o'clock next morning Massena carried the village of Porço Velho: the light division and cavalry were sent to support General Houston; at the same time the first and third divisions moved to their right. The Guards were thrown back *en potence*.

The enemy's cavalry supported by the infantry and artillery, drove in part of the seventh division. Don Julian Sanchez left Nava d'Aver with his men, and placed himself immediately in front of the Guards: here his lieutenant was unfortunately shot by a soldier of the Coldstream, who mistook him for a Frenchman.

Some advantageous ground on which the English cavalry were stationed being abandoned, was instantly seized by the French, The light division then advanced to support the cavalry, but, finding the height occupied, formed into squares, and retired in good order, repelling all the efforts of the hostile cavalry to force them; the *Chasseurs Britanniques* under Lieutenant-Colonel Eustace, also distinguished themselves by the steady manner in which they repulsed the enemy's dragoons. The Allies were concentrated towards the left, on the seventh, the light divisions and cavalry moving on Fuentes d'Honor. The two remaining divisions followed in succession.

Wellington now found himself obliged to abandon his communication across the Coa by the bridge of Sabugal. The position extended along the height from Turon to the Duas Casas. The first division was on the right, in two lines; Colonel Ashworth's brigade in the centre; and the third division, also in two lines, on the left. The village of Fuentes d'Honor, in their front, was occupied by the light troops. The light division and cavalry were in reserve.

May the fifth, the infantry of Don Julian joined the seventh division in Freynada. The French cavalry advanced in mass under a heavy cannonade to within a short distance of the line where the Guards were formed, when the brigade of nine-pounders under Captain Lawson opened, and obliged the enemy to halt. After a few rounds of grape, they went about in great confusion. The piquets of the first division, under Lieutenant-Colonel Hill of the Third Guards, succeeded in repulsing a charge of the enemy's cavalry; but in making their way to the cover of the army they were again attacked and broken before any force could be sent to their assistance.

Lieutenant-Colonel Hill was taken prisoner, others were wounded, and the party was overpowered. The French throughout the day were unremitting in their attacks on Fuentes d'Honor, where several regiments and officers greatly distinguished themselves. On one occasion the Seventy-First, Seventy-Ninth, and Eighty-Eighth regiments,

Battle of
FUENTES D'ONORE
5th. May, 1811.

Allies   French

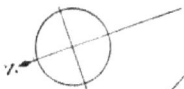

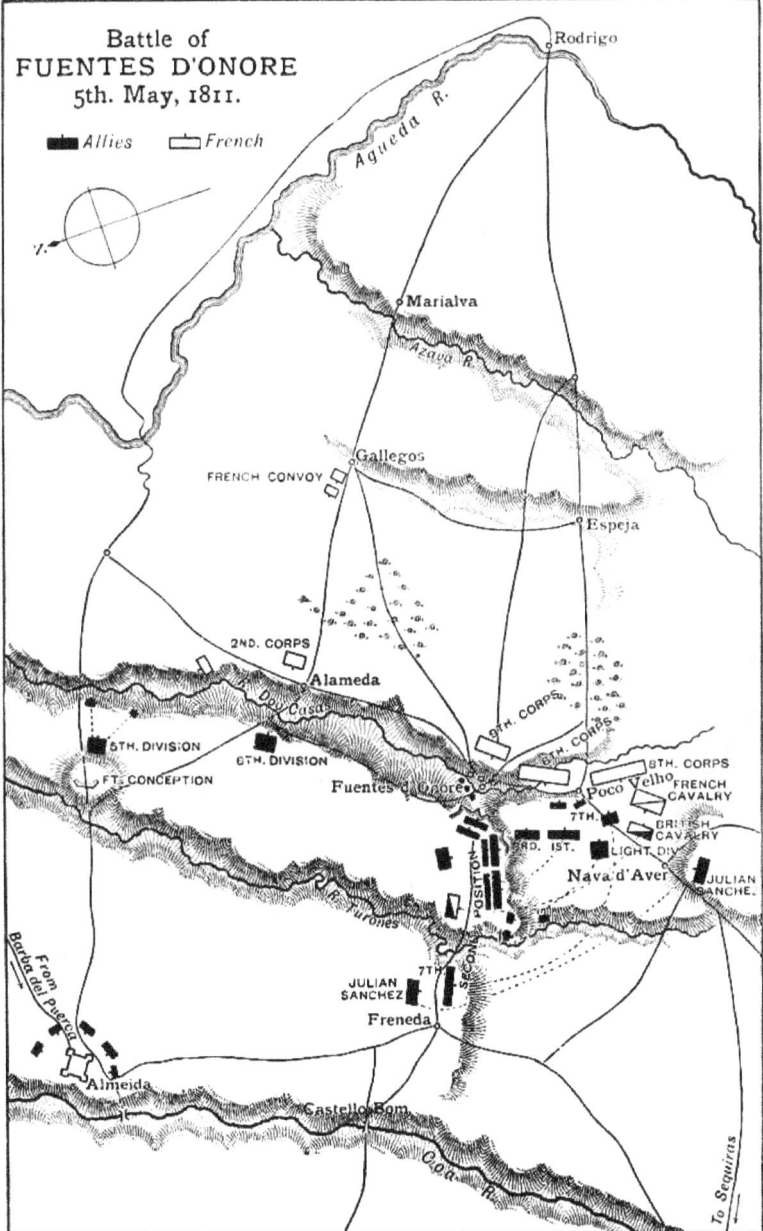

Rodrigo

Agueda R.

Marialva

Azava R.

Gallegos

FRENCH CONVOY

Espeja

2ND. CORPS

Alameda

R. dos Casas

9TH. CORPS

6TH. CORPS

8TH. CORPS

5TH. DIVISION

6TH. DIVISION

FT. CONCEPTION

Fuentes d'Onore

Poco Velho   FRENCH CAVALRY

7TH

3RD. 1ST.

BRITISH CAVALRY

LIGHT DIV.

Nava d'Aver

JULIAN SANCHE.

SECOND POSITION

R. Turones

From Barba del Puerca

JULIAN SANCHEZ   7TH

Freneda

Almeida

Castello Bom

Coa R.

To Sequiros

Walker & Boutall sc.

belonging to Colonel Henry Mackinnon's brigade, were ordered up. Led by that officer, they gallantly charged a heavy mass of infantry that had gained the chapel eminence, and drove the French through the village with great slaughter. The contest lasted till night, when the fire gradually slackened; the upper part of the village was retained by the British, and the enemy made no further attempt.

★★★★★★

The Ninety-Second regiment arrived on the position at Fuentes d'Honor much distressed from want of provisions; which circumstance being made known to the brigade of Guards, they volunteered giving up a ration of biscuit, then in their haversacks, which was received by the gallant Highlanders with three hearty cheers.

★★★★★★

The casualties in the Coldstream were, four rank and file killed; Captain Harvey, two sergeants, and forty-nine rank and file wounded; Ensign Stothert and seven rank and file taken. (The loss of the Allies amounted to about fifteen hundred; three hundred of whom were made prisoners. The enemy's loss greatly exceeded that of their opponents.)

Massena was recalled to France, and the Duke of Ragusa, who had been appointed to the command of the Army of Portugal in his steady arrived from Paris on the seventh of May. On the same day the French retreated. A loud explosion was heard at twelve o'clock on the night of the eleventh, General Brennier the *commandant* of Almeida having sprung a mine in order to facilitate his escape with the garrison, consisting of about fifteen hundred men. This he accomplished by a sudden and well-conducted movement.

General Pack, who commanded the investing piquets, hastily collected some troops end followed, keeping up a constant fire on the rear of the French, which was not returned; neither did they slacken their pace, but marched across the country, protected by the darkness of the night, and descended the valley of Barba del Puerco, They lost many men, but their main body succeeded in reaching the bridge on the Coa, where they found the second French corps drawn up in order of battle to cover them. (The French lost three hundred men, killed, wounded, and taken.)

Having assumed the command May 7th, Marmont retired towards Salamanca, in the neighbourhood of which town his army was placed in cantonments.

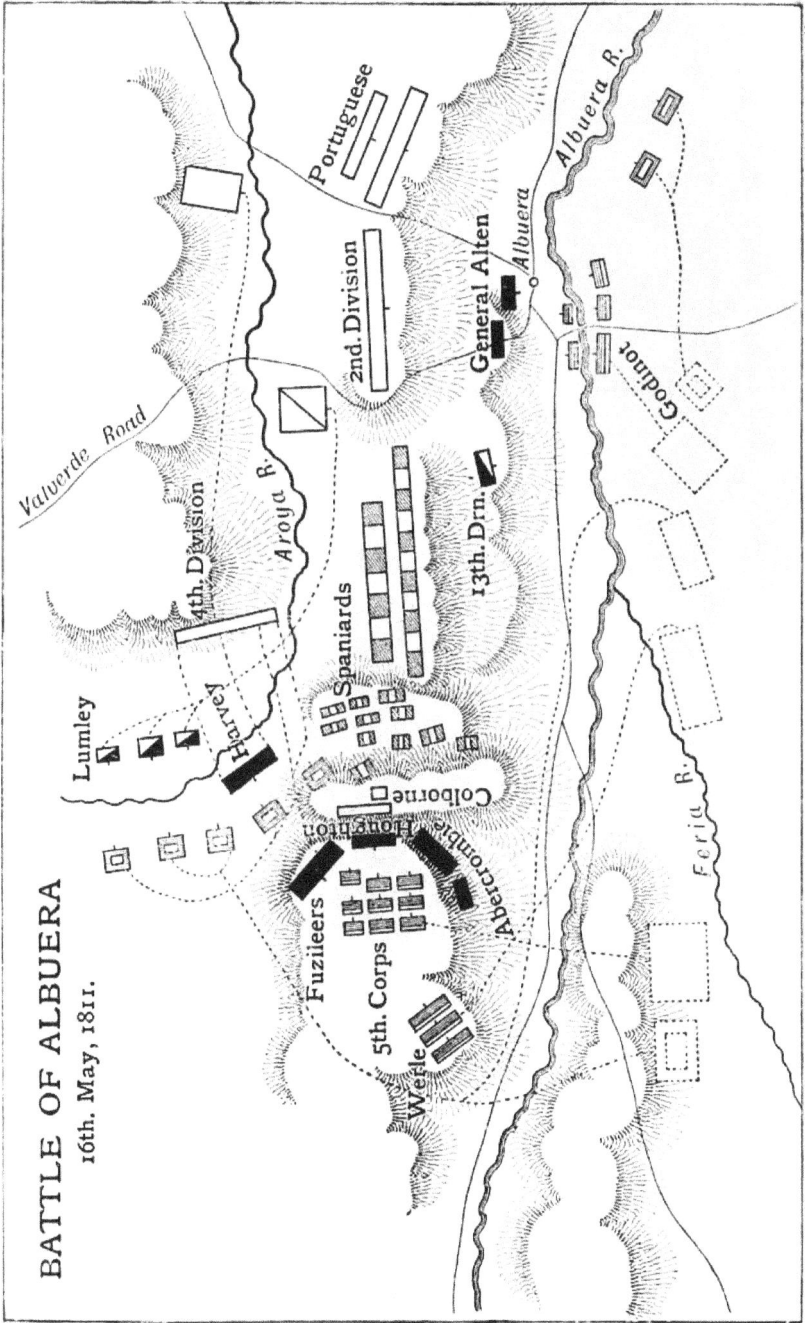

BATTLE OF ALBUERA
16th. May, 1811.

On the eleventh the Guards returned to the places they had occupied previous to the action. The fifth, sixths and light divisions were left on the Agueda and Coa. The first division moved from their cantonments and marched in the evening of the twenty-fifth through Soita to Penamacor, whence the Guards were ordered to go back to their former stations, part of the division only being required in the south. The Guards returned on the 27th through Sabugal, and arrived at Almadilla and Puebla, May 29th.

Beresford had on the eighth of May completely invested Badajoz.

Marshal Soult left Seville with the intention of succouring the town; on his march he was reinforced with fresh troops.

Beresford in consequence raised the siege and advanced meet him, when it was agreed with Blake, who commanded the Spaniards in this direction, that the Allied army should take up a position at the village of Albuera, and Beresford, though junior, was allowed to take the command-in-chief *pro tempore*. They occupied the position, (May 15th,) with nearly thirty thousand infantry, of which seven thousand only were British, two thousand cavalry, and thirty-eight pieces of artillery,

Soult's force consisted of twenty thousand infantry, three thousand cavalry, and forty guns. The Allies remained masters of the field. As the Guards took no part at Albuera, a description of that battle is not here inserted. It may, however, be remarked, that Lord Beresford's conduct throughout the day proved him to merit that character and consideration in the army, which he has always maintained.

The intrepidity of the British infantry, on whom the brunt of the battle fell, was conspicuously displayed in this action. Fifteen hundred men only remained out of seven thousand. The loss of the French was also very considerable.

Wellington learnt, by an intercepted letter, on the tenth of June, that Marmont intended to unite with Soult in the Alentejo. The siege of Badajoz, which had been renewed after the Battle of Albuera, was in consequence of this information converted into a blockade.

The Coldstream left Puebla on the fifth for Almadilla; next day the brigade of Guards marched from that place with the corps under Spencer, and moved from the north in a parallel direction with Marmont, passing Sabugal and Castello Branco.

They then crossed the Tagus and proceeded to Portalegre, where the Coldstream halted three days. On the twenty-third of June they encamped near St, Oloia, when, to protect them from the great heat, the troops were hutted. A draft joined the regiment from Cadiz on the twenty-fifth, consisting of Captain the Honourable John Walpole, Ensign Greville, three sergeants, and ninety-eight rank and file; soon after the first division was reviewed by Lord Wellington, accompanied by the Prince of Orange,

Soult returned to Seville, and Marmont advanced to Salamanca, being unable to provide supplies for their army when together.

Hill's corps remained in the Alentejo, July 22nd. The brigade of Guards left St. Oloia, reached Portalegre the twenty-third, and on the thirty-first received orders to return to the north. Lord Wellington re-crossed the Tagus with the rest of the army, and fixed his headquarters at Fuente Guinaldo.

On the sixth of September, General Graham succeeded Sir Brent Spencer in the command of the first division.

Lord Wellington blockaded Ciudad Rodrigo; on the approach of Marmont he retired, and occupied a defensive position. The British general was not prepared to besiege the place; his object being to oblige the enemy to withdraw from Galicia and Navarre, and thus give relief to those oppressed provinces.

General Picton was in advance on the height of El Bodon, between Fuente Guinaldo and Pastore., The light division was near Martiago. The left wing, in which were the Guards, was in the lower Azava. Sir Stapleton Cotton with the cavalry was in the centre.

Marmont joined his forces with General Dorsenne on the twenty-second of September, and relieved Ciudad Rodrigo: he entered the place with a large convoy on the twenty-fourth. The French advanced two days after in great force, and obliged the Allies to retreat. Next day the village of Aldea de Ponte was attacked by the enemy, and gallantly contested by the fourth division.

After dark the British again retreated, and took up a strong position behind the Soito. Here Wellington offered the enemy battle, but Marmont fell back on Ciudad Rodrigo; and Dorsenne returned to the north. The Allied army then went into cantonments in October. The brigade of Guards was stationed in front of Celerico; the Coldstream at Lagoisa, Valdozares, and afterwards at Pinhel. The headquarters were at Freynada.

General Hill left Portalegre on the twenty-second of October, and after three days reached Malpartida. The next evening, he made a forced march to Acuesa, and silently waited till morning, when he surprised a post under General Girard at Arroyo de Molinos, which was carried at the point of the bayonet. Many men were killed, and fifteen hundred taken, besides General Brun and the Duke d'Aremberg, with all their artillery, stores, and baggage.

This was a brilliant exploit, and in itself of sufficient moment to establish a claim to military eminence. The reputation of Hill, however, does not rest on a solitary act of courage or skilful generalship: his name will descend to posterity interwoven with the triumphs of Wellington.

RETURN OF OFFICERS OF THE FIRST BATTALION OF THE COLDSTREAM FOR THE YEAR 1811.

	Officers present in the Peninsula.	From	To			Officers absent.	Cause of absence.	From	To
Lt.-C.	Joseph Fuller	March	31 Dec.		Lt.-G.	John Calcraft, 1st Major	Leave	1 Jan.	31 Dec.
,,	Hon. H. Brand	1 Jan.	April		Col.	Richard Hulse	Commanding a Brigade	,,	,,
,,	James Philips	,,	31 Dec.		,,	H. Mac Kinnon	Do. Sick leave	4 July	3 July Dec.
,,	Sir G. Stirling, Bart.	,,	,,		,,	W. M. Peacocke	Commandant at Lisbon	1 Jan.	31 Dec.
,,	George Smyth	,,	3 July		M.-G.	W. P. Acland	On the Staff at home.	,,	,,
,,	Thomas Braddyl	Oct.	3 Dec.		Col.	M. Lord Aylmer	Asst. Adjt. Genl. Portugal. Sick leave to England	,, 12 July	11 July Dec.
Capt.	E.Dalling,(Maj.)	1 Jan.	31 July		Lt.Cl.	Hon. H. Brand	Posted to 2d Batt.	April	
,,	L. F. Adams, (Major)	,,	31 Dec.		,,	George Smyth	Leave to England on resignation.	4 July	
,,	George Collier	,,	3 Dec.		,,	R. D. Jackson	Asst. Qur. Mr. Genl. Portugal	March	31 Dec.
,,	Sir H. Sullivan, Bart.	,,	Nov.		,,	Thos. Braddyl	Leave to England on resignation	4 Dec.	
,,	W. H. Raikes	,,	31 Dec.		,,	H. F. Bouverie	Acting Milr. Secy. Portugal	Jan.	31 Dec.
,,	H. W. Vachell	,,	Sept.		Capt.	Edward Dalling	Died 31st July		
,,	Thomas Barrow	,,	31 Dec.		,,	George Collier	Promoted in 2d Batt.	4 Dec.	
,,	Hon. W. Geo. Crofton	Feb.	,,		,,	H. F. Cooke	Deputy Asst. Adjt. Genl. Portugal Leave to England	1 Jan. 18 Sept.	17 Sept. 31 Dec.
,,	D. Mac Kinnon	1 Jan.	15 Aug.		,,	Sir H. Sullivan, Bart.	Sick leave to Lisbon	Nov.	,,
,,	Hon. J. Walpole	25 June	31 Dec.		,,	H. W. Vachell	Promoted in 2d Batt.	Sept.	
,,	Thomas Steele	Feb.	,,		,,	D. Mac Kinnon	A.D.C. to Hon. E. Stopford Sick leave to England	June 16 Aug.	15 Aug. 31 Dec.
,,	Edward Harvey	March	,,		,,	Henry Dawkins	Brigade Major Portugal	1 Jan.	31 Dec.
,,	George Bowles	Oct.	,,		,,	J. V. Harvey	Promoted in 2d Batt.	1 April	,,
,,	Thomas Sowerby	Nov.	,,		,,	W. L. Walton	Ditto.	24 ,,	,,
,,	James V. Harvey	1 Jan.	30 Mar.		Ens.	W. Lockwood	Leave to England. Resigned	23 May	
Ens.	W. L. Walton	,,	23 April		,,	Hon. J.Wingfield	Died 4th May		
,,	W. Lockwood	,,	22 May		Capt.	P. St. J. Mild-may	Promoted in 2d Batt.	1 Dec.	,,
,,	Hon. J.Wingfield	,,	4 May		,,	A. Wedderburn	Ditto	Dec.	,,
,,	Paulet St. John Mildmay	,,	30 Nov.		Ens.	W. Stothert	Taken prisoner at Fuentes d'Honor	5 May	,,
,,	A. Wedderburn	,,	Dec.						
,,	Charles White	,,	31 Dec.						
,,	Thomas Bligh	,,	,,						
,,	Charles Shawe	,,	,,						
,,	G. H. M. Greville	25 June	,,						
,,	John Talbot	Oct.	,,						
,,	G. H. Percival	1 Jan.	,,						
,,	William Stothert	,,	5 May						
,,	W. G. Baynes	,,	31 Dec.						
,,	John S. Cowell	,,	,,						
,,	W. N. Burgess	Feb.	,,						
,,	John Mills	Jan.	,,						
,,	James Bradshaw	March	,,						
,,	F. L. Beckford	Oct.	,,						
,,	Fred. Vachell	,,	,,						
Adjt.	J. Freemantle (Capt.)	1 Jan.	,,						
Q-Mr.	John Holmes	,,	,,						
Surg.	Charles Coombe	,,	,,						
Asst Sur.	Thomas Rose	,,	,,						
,,	Edward Nixon	March	,,						

STRENGTH OF THE FIRST BATTALION OF THE COLD-STREAM AT PINHEL, 25th December, 1811.

Capts. and Lieut.-Cols.	Lieutenants and Capts.	Ensigns.	Adjutant.	Q.-Master.	Surgeon.	Assistant Surgeons.	Staff employ and otherwise absent.			Absent without leave.	Commission vacant.	Serjeants.	Drummers.	Rank and File.	Sick.	On Command.	Total.
							Capts. and Lt.-Cols.	Lieuts. and Capts.	Ensigns.								
4	11	13	1	1	1	2	6	3	2	One Sub.	One Ens.	69	22	744	144	61	1086

	Officers present.		Officers absent	Cause of absence.
Col.	1. J. Fuller	M.-Gen.	R. Hulse	1. Staff, Portugal
Lt.-Col.	2. J. Philips	,,	H. Mac Kinnon	2. Ditto
,,	3. Sir G. Stirling	,,	W. M. Peacocke	3. Ditto
Capt.	1. L. F. Adams, (Major)	Col.	M. Lord Aylmer	4. Asst. Adjt.-Gen. ditto
,,	6. Hon. J. Walpole	Lt.-Col.	R. D. Jackson	5. Asst.Q.-Master-Gen. ditto
,,	7. T. Steele	,,	4. A. Woodford	On the march from Lisbon to join
,,	8. E. Harvey	,,	H. F. Bouverie	6. Taken on from 2d battalion
,,	9. G. Bowles	Capt.	F. Sutton	1. Taken on from 2d battalion
,,	10. T. Sowerby	,,	E. Lascelles	3. With 2d battalion
Ensign	1. C. White	,,	3. W. H. Raikes	Sick at Val dos Ayres
,,	3. C. Shawe	,,	D. Mac Kinnon	In England
,,	4. G. H. M. Greville	,,	H. Dawkins	2. Brigade-Major, Portugal
,,	5. J. Talbot	,,	11. A. Wedderburn	On duty at Lisbon: belonging to 2d battalion
,,	6. G. H. Percjval	,,	4. T. Barrow	On the road to join from sick, absent
,,	8. J. S. Cowell	,,	2. Sir H. Sullivan	Leave for 6 weeks to Lisbon
,,	9. W. N. Burgess	,,	5. Hon. W. G. Crofton	Leave for 6 weeks to Lisbon
,,	10. J. Mills			On the road to join from sick, absent
,,	11. J. Bradshaw	Ensign	2. T. Bligh	On duty at Coimbra
,,	12. F.L. Beckford	,,	7. W. G. Baynes	Leave for 1 month to Lisbon
Adjutant	J. Freemantle, (Capt.)	,,	13. F. Vachell	1. With 2d. bat.
Q.-Mastr.	J. Holmes	,,	J. L. Blackman	2. Prisoner of war
Asst. Surg.	T. Rose	,,	W. Stothert	Sick at Val dos Ayres
,,	E. Nixon	Surgeon	C. Coombe	To join 2d battalion
		Capt.	P. St.J. Mildmay	To England on promotion
		Lt.-Col.	G. Collier	To England on resignation.
		,,	T. Braddyll	

(Signed)   CHARLES STEWART,
M.-G. and A.-G.

117

CHAPTER 9

Battle of Salamanca

Marmont having detached four divisions of his army, besides the one under General Dubreton, stationed in the province of Las Montanas, Wellington determined at once to lay siege to Ciudad Rodrigo.

On the sixth, headquarters were transferred to Gallegos; but from a fall of snow and the inclemency of the weather, the army did not move till the eighth, when General Craufurd's division crossed the Agueda, and invested the town. After dark Lieutenant-Colonel Colborne with a detachment of the light division stormed and carried an advanced redoubt on the great Teson.

Sir Thomas Graham was intrusted with the direction of the siege. From the eighth instant the Coldstream was quartered at Espeja. The brigade of Guards formed the working party in the trenches on the ninth, on which night the first parallel was established and the several batteries marked out. The Guards were also in the trenches on the thirteenth, when a fortified convent, situated on the right of the redoubt before taken, was carried by the light infantry companies, supported by Lord Blantyre's brigade.

The garrison made a sortie on the fourteenth, and were repulsed without effecting any injury except filling in a part of the sap. In the evening the batteries opened, and the convent of St. Francisco, which flanked the approaches on the left, was escaladed and carried by the Fortieth regiment.

On the seventeenth the Guards again took their turn in the trenches.

The second parallel was completed; but Wellington determined to order an assault the moment the breaches were deemed practicable, without waiting for the opening of the sap to blow in the counterscarp; and as every exertion was made, two breaches were completed on the nineteenth. General Picton's division was directed to storm the greater breach, and General Craufurd's the smaller. After dark the columns moved forward, and in less than an hour the British were formed on the ramparts.

General Craufurd was mortally wounded whilst leading his division up the glacis. General Mackinnon was killed, with many others, by the unfortunate explosion of an expense magazine after a shower of grape and musketry, and just as the troops had pushed on and cleared the breach.

The Allies lost during the siege and in the storming about one thousand three hundred men. Seventy-eight officers and seventeen hundred men of the French were made prisoners, besides a heavy loss in killed and wounded

The capture of a complete battering train, with magazines filled with shot, shells, muskets, cartridges, and other ammunition, was the result of this success.

As soon as Ciudad Rodrigo was again placed in a state of defence and supplied with stores and provisions, Wellington planned his arrangements for the reduction of Badajoz, The army in consequence was put in movement for the south: in February no British troops remained on the Agueda or at any point north of the Tagus. Trant occupied the line of the Coa and its vicinity; his orders were to watch Marmont on the frontier, and also to cover the magazines at Celerico.

The first division left their quarters and passed through Sabugal to Castello Branco. The Coldstream, after halting one day, continued their route by Abrantes to Elvas. At the latter place the division encamped close to the town, when tents were furnished the men for the first time. On the sixteenth they broke up, and the brigade of Guards crossed the Guadiana over a pontoon bridge below the town of Badajoz, which was thus invested by the third, fourth, and light divisions, under Beresford. General Graham advanced with the first, sixth, and seventh divisions, and two brigades of cavalry, towards Llerena; whilst General Hill's corps moved from their cantonments near Albuquerque to Merida: the enemy on their approach retired to Cordova.

The siege of Badajoz was prosecuted without intermission, although torrents of rain had swept away the pontoon bridge; and from the rapidity of the current, the flying bridges could only be worked with great difficulty. These obstacles occasioned supplies of all descriptions to be kept back; and the trenches on the low ground were filled with water.

Soult advanced with a large force to the relief of the town. Graham and Hill then retired on Albuera.

The second parallel was formed; enfilading and breaching batteries had been erected; and on the sixth of April, after the firing had been kept up seven days, three breaches were deemed practicable. At ten o'clock p.m. simultaneous attacks were made; the first that succeeded was that of Picton's division, led by General Kemp. General Walker, with his brigade, also entered by escalade on the Olivença road. General Philippon, the commandant, escaped to St. Christoval, a fort on the opposite side of the Guadiana, which shortly after surrendered. The number of prisoners taken in Badajoz amounted to nearly four thousand: the loss of the Allies from the commencement of the siege was about five thousand men.

Wellington left Hill's corps on the south of the Tagus, and put his army in motion for the north.

During the siege of Badajoz, Marmont had advanced as far as Castello Branco; but, informed of Wellington's movement, he retreated towards Ciudad Rodrigo, and having raised the blockade of that place, retired on Salamanca.

In May, headquarters were again established at Fuente Guinaldo, and the troops cantoned between the Agueda and Coa.

Previous to entering Spain, May 12th, Lord Wellington had ordered General Hill to move by Zaraceijo, for the purpose of destroying the bridge of boats across the Tagus, at Almarez, which, if effected, would render the communication between the enemy's armies on the north mud south of the Tagus more difficult. All the permanent bridges had been destroyed during the war by one or other of the belligerent powers. The bridge at Almarez was covered at each extremity by strong works, besides being protected on the south by the castle and redoubts of Miravete. From the difficulty of approach, it was not till daybreak on the nineteenth of May that an attack could be made.

The right column then moved to the assault of Fort Napoleon, on the left bank of the river. The British rushed on with fixed bayonets, and drove the enemy over the bridge: so great was the panic, that the troops in Fort Ragusa, on the right bank, abandoned their works, and fled in disorder. Eighteen guns, and two hundred and fifty men, were taken. The British loss was under two hundred. Hill afterwards returned to Almandrelejo.

On June 17th, the army left their cantonments on the Agueda, and forded the Tormes above and below Salamanca. Two forts, constructed by the enemy, could only be reduced by a regular attack: the sixth division, under Major-General Clinton, was therefore selected for this duty; and the rest of the army was kept in readiness to check the enemy, who were anxious to hold a communication with the forts. An attempt to carry the principal fort, St. Vincente, failed. Major-General Bowes, and one hundred and twenty men, were killed,

Marmont made a forward movement on the twentieth, and found the Allies posted on the height of St. Christoval; their right resting on the Tormes near Carbrerizos, their left near Villares de la Reyna: a skirmish took place with the cavalry. During the night of the twenty-first the enemy established themselves on the right flank of the position; from which they were afterwards dislodged by the seventh division, June 17th.

On the night of the twenty-third Marmont crossed the Tormes in great force; but finding that the first, sixths and seventh divisions, under Graham, had also forded the river with some cavalry and artillery, he returned and re-occupied his former ground.

A few days after, June 27th, the largest of the forts, which had been battered with red-hot shot, was seen to be on fire.

The men were formed ready for an assault, when a proposition was made to capitulate in three hours; in reply to which Wellington gave them five minutes to march out, promising them their baggage. The garrison not taking advantage of the offer, the storming party advanced, under Lieutenant-Colonel Davies of the Thirty-Sixth regiment: the small fort was carried, and the attack on St. Vincente had commenced, when the *commandant* accepted the proposed terms. About seven hundred men were made prisoners, the works blown up, and the captured guns, with the stores, given to the Spaniards. The Allies lost four hundred and fifty men killed and wounded.

After the capture of these forts in July, Marmont retreated behind the Douro, where he concentrated his forces, his centre resting on Tordesillas.

Wellington established his headquarters at Rueda, and his line extended from La Seca to Pollos.

The French had been reinforced on the seventh by General Bonnet, with eight thousand men; and their present position being most advantageous, Marmont resolved on becoming the assailant. On the sixteenth large bodies crossed the river at Toro: the same evening the British troops moved to Fuente la Peña and Carnizal, on the Guarena, The next day it was ascertained that the enemy had recrossed the

Douro, and were again concentrated at Tordesillas, at which place their army crossed the river, and assembled at Nave del Rey Castrejon.

July 18th, Marmont had now opened his communication with the army of the centre, which was on its march from Madrid to support him: his present object was to prevent the Allies from having any intercourse with Salamanca and Ciudad Rodrigo.

On the twenty-first the Allies concentrated on the Tormes, having repulsed the enemy on the eighteenth, who had attempted to turn their left and gain the valley of Carnizal.

Between Huerta and Alba de Tormes the French crossed the river, pressing forward their left to gain the Ciudad Rodrigo road, Wellington also crossed by the bridge at Salamanca, and before daylight next morning both armies were in position; the right of the Allies extending nearly to the steep heights called the Sister Arapiles; their left resting on the Tormes, The enemy's front was covered by a wood.

At daybreak on the twenty-second much skirmishing took place. A French column advanced about eight o'clock, and seized the farthest and most extensive height. The British troops immediately took possession of the other. Some changes were then made in the arrangements of the Allied army, and a succession of manoeuvre on the part of the enemy showed that it was Marmont's intention to turn the right of the Allies.

Probably against a less skilful general than Wellington he might have succeeded. But in making this attempt, which was covered by a constant skirmish and cannonade along the whole fronts he pushed his left too far, and weakened his centre; the moment was seized by Wellington, who instantly determined to attack.

At this time the first and light divisions formed the left, the fourth and fifth drawn up in two lines behind the village of Arapiles; the sixth and seventh, and the Spaniards under Don Carlos de España, were in column for their support. On the right was the division of Major-General Pakenham, with the greater part of the cavalry.

The village of Arapiles, which the enemy made repeated efforts to carry, was situated between the two armies, and was occupied by the light companies of the Guards under Lieutenant-Colonel Woodford of the Coldstream. Pakenham advanced to the attack with the third division in columns of battalions, when they wheeled to the left, supported by General D'Urban's brigade of Portuguese cavalry: on reaching the height General Pakenham deployed, his right outflanking the enemy's left. He then advanced, and carried everything at the point of the bayonet.

The cavalry made a successful charge in front; during which General Le Marchant was killed. General Pack, with the Portuguese brigade, failed more than once to carry the Arapiles; the enemy, after repulsing them, advanced from the height, and suddenly attacked the left of the fourth division; the disorder this occasioned was checked by the advance of part of the fifth. The third and fourth divisions then moved forward, and crowned the height.

The last stand was made by the enemy on their right, who attempted to rally, their troops having retired in good order from the Arapiles. Clinton's division was ordered to attack in front, supported by the third and fifth divisions; the fourth making at the same time a flank movement on the left.

Clinton, in this advance, suffered severely from the fire of the artillery and musketry; but he steadily persevered till within a short distance of the enemy, on whom his troops rushed with the bayonet, when the fourth division appearing, the French quitted their position in great disorder. The first and light divisions followed in pursuit from sun-set till the troops halted from fatigue, July 22nd. The French crossed the Tormes the same night at Alba.

Their loss must have been very great; besides killed and wounded, seven thousand were made prisoners. Lord Wellington, in his dispatch, states that eleven guns were left in possession of the Allies; several others were afterwards found, making a total of not less than twenty. The loss on the part of the Allies was five thousand two hundred. In the Coldstream the casualties were principally from the light company. Ensign Hotham was wounded; one sergeant, two corporals, and four privates were killed; three sergeants, one corporal, one drummer, and seventeen privates were wounded; eight men also were missing.

The following is an extract from Lord Wellington's dispatch:—

I must also, mention Lieutenant-Colonel Woodford, commanding the light battalion of the brigade of Guards, who, supported by two companies of the fusiliers, under the command of Captain Crowder, maintained the village of Arapiles against all the efforts of the enemy.

At this time the colossal power of Napoleon had brought half the population of Christendom under his sway. He now resolved to undertake an expedition into Russia. The French Army marched in ten corps, under Davoust, Oudinot, Ney, Eugene Beauharnais, Ponia-

Battle of
SALAMANCA
with operations
before and after the Action.

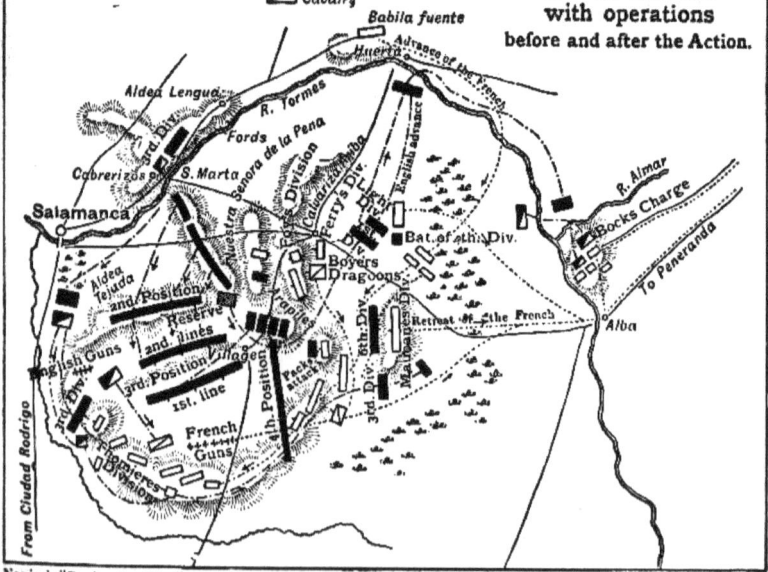

To Benavente
R. Esla
Castromonte
General Durban
Ribeira Fresno
Zamora
Duero R.
Toro
Tordesillas
Hornillo
Castro-nuno
Fuentel Sauco
Alaejos
Castrillo
St. Olfio
Canizal
Cabeza Velosa
St. Christoval
Aldea Rubia
Tormes R.
Salamanca
Ft. Ciudad
Voltusra R.
La Serna
Huerta
Arapiles
Alba
Ventosa
Nava Setroval
Peneranda
Valesa
Cantalpiro
Cantalapiedra
Torrecilla
Orden
Tarazona
Cisla
Flores d'Avila
Fontiveros
Brasco Sancho
Blasco Sancho
Castrejon
Zagorcial R.
Navadel Rey
Rueda
Pollos
Medina del Campo
Olmedo
Arevalo
Simancas
Valladolid
To Duenas
R. Pisuerga
Esqueva R.
Tudela
Duera R.
Bocill
Fuente Duero
To Aranda
Cuellar
Eresma R.
S. Maria
Segovia
Adaja R.
Espinar
Avila
Escurial
Guadarrama

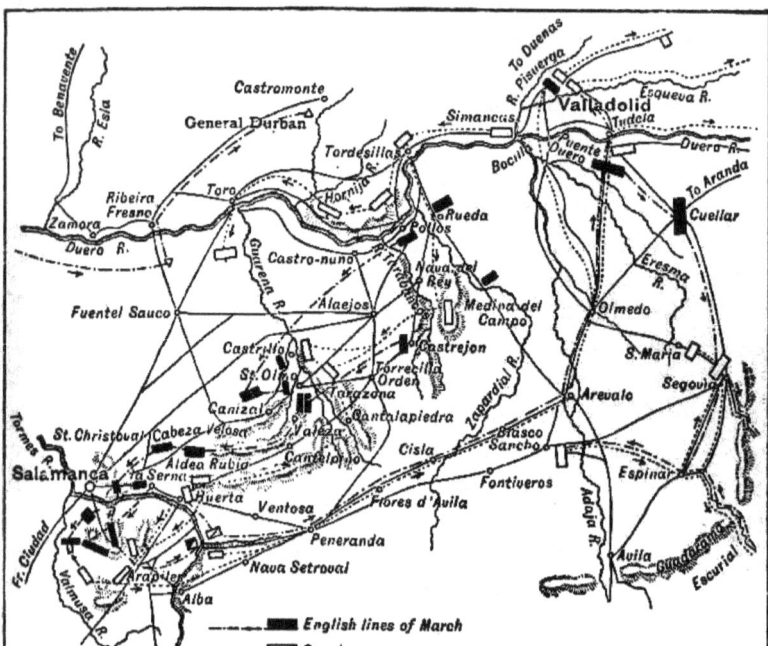

English lines of March
Cavalry
French lines of March
Cavalry

Babila fuente
Advance of the French
Huerta
Aldea Lengua
R. Tormes
Fords
Sonora de la Pena
Cabrerizos
S. Marta
Salamanca
Division
Clara
Condrizancha
English advance
Pack's Div.
Clinton's Div.
Cole's Div.
Pack's Div.
Terry's Div.
Bat. of 5th. Div.
Boyers Dragoons
Aldea Tejuda
2nd. Position
Reserve
3rd. lines
3rd. Position
Village
1st. line
5th Position
English Guns
French Guns
Retreat of the French
3rd. Div.
5th. Div.
Maucune
R. Almar
Bocks Charge
To Peneranda
Alba
Pack's attack
Boyers Bivouac
From Ciudad Rodrigo

towski, Gouvion St. Cyr, Regnier, Junot, Victor, and Macdonald. The bodyguard was under Le Fevre, and the young guard under Mortier. The reserve of the cavalry, commanded by the King of Naples, was in four bodies, under Nansouty, Montbrun, Grouchy, and Latour Maubourg. The cavalry of the Guard, as well as the Austrian force, acted separately. This army is said to have exceeded four hundred and seventy-five thousand men, besides one hundred thousand auxiliaries. It perished miserably among the snows of Russia.

The Duke of Ragusa having been wounded, the command devolved on General Clausel, who retreated to Valladolid, followed by the British, which town the latter entered on the thirteenth; but as the French general continued his retreat to Burgos, Wellington determined to march against the army of the centre, and for this purpose repassed the Douro. After remaining some days at Cuellar, August 7th he moved by Segovia to Madrid, leaving some, troops under General Paget near the Douro.

King Joseph had quitted Madrid on the twenty-first of July to unite with Marmont; but hearing of that general's defeat on the twenty-fifth near Airivole, he retreated on Segovia, with the expectation that Wellington would follow, hoping to draw his attention from Clausel. On the first of August Joseph fell back, leaving behind him some dragoons, who were defeated by General D'Urban's Portuguese brigade of cavalry.

The Allies entered Madrid on the twelfth, and were received with great enthusiasm by the population.

Joseph, with the army of the centre, had retired from the Capital on the preceding evenings taking the road to Toledo, leaving about seventeen hundred men at Fort La China, in the palace of the Retiro, who surrendered next day.

On the twenty-fifth the French abandoned their works opposite Cadiz and the Isla. Two days afterwards the combined force, under General La Cruza and Colonel Skerret, entered Seville.

Here the enemy attempted to defend the bridge, but the grenadiers of the First Guards charged with the bayonet, and put them to flight; several of their number were left dead in the streets, and more than two hundred prisoners were taken, with a quantity of baggage, horses, and money.

The first division of the Allied army left Madrid, and was quartered in the palace of the Escurial with the fourth, fifth, and sixth divisions.

King Joseph joined Suchet in Valencia; Soult was in Granada.

With the exception of one battalion, all the English had marched from Cadiz. General Hill, who was at Truxillo, intended to advance on Oropesa, to act in concert with the army under Wellington.

On the first of September Wellington left Madrid, and entered Valladolid, where the Guards remained a few days, and marched to Burgos, the castle of which, strongly defended by fieldworks bristled with cannon, commanded the river. The place was invested on the night of the nineteenth, and the siege intrusted to the first and sixth divisions.

During the night a detachment from the Forty-Second regiment stormed and carried a horn work on the hill of St. Michael, which covered the lower wall of the castle. Next day batteries were erected on this hill.

In the night of the twenty-second the besiegers endeavoured to escalade and establish themselves on the outer wall and first line of fieldworks; they failed however in the attempt, and retired with considerable loss, (Sept. 29th).

A week after a mine was exploded: working parties had been constantly in the trenches constructing batteries, but the breach was not deemed practicable. Early in October, the commander of the forces had occasion to notice in orders the misconduct of several of these working parties, but at the same time observed, that:

> He was happy to make an exception in favour of the Guards, who, he is informed, have invariably performed this duty, as they have every other in this army, in the most exemplary manner.

A second breach was made on the evening of the fourth, and a lodgement effected between the outer wall and the first line of fieldworks; but the garrison drove back the British, who however, on being reinforced, obliged the French to retire behind their defences. Before daylight on the eighth the garrison made a rush, overthrew the guard, and destroyed all the works between the second line and outer wall. Another and last attempt was made on the eighteenth, but the heavy fire from the garrison rendered it impossible for the assailants to maintain their ground.

The loss of the Allies during the siege exceeded two thousand, which was about equal to that of the garrison.

★★★★★★

CASUALTIES IN THE COLDSTREAM.

Killed, &c. in the assault and capture of Fort St. Michael on the 19th of September, 1812; wounded, 1 sergeant, 2 rank and file.

Killed, &c. in the siege of the Castle of Burgos, from the 20th to the 26th of September inclusive—Killed, 13 rank and file; wounded, 1 captain, 2 sergeants, 39 rank and file. Wounded, Capt. Fraser.

From 27th Sept. to 3rd October—Killed, 1 sergeant, 2 rank and file; wounded, 8 rank and file.

From 4th to 6th October—Killed, 1 rank and file; wounded, 6 *do.*

From 6th to 10th October—Killed, 1 ensign, 11 rank and file; wounded, 27 rank and file, and one missing. Killed, Ensign Buckeridge.

From 11th to 17th October—Killed, 3 rank and file; wounded, 1 *do.*

From 18th to 21st October—Killed, 1 captain, 1 ensign, 1 sergeant, 22 rank and file; wounded, 2 captains, 1 sergeant, 32 rank and file. Capt, Edward Harvey killed; Ensign Burgess killed; Hon. W. G. Crofton and Hon. John Walpole wounded.

✶✶✶✶✶✶

The following is an extract of a dispatch, dated "Cabeçon, October 26th, 1812," detailing the operations against the castle of Burgos on the eighteenth of October;

It is impossible to represent in adequate terms my sense of the conduct of the Guards and German Legion upon this occasion; and I am quite satisfied, that if it had been possible to maintain the posts which they had gained with so much gallantry, these troops would have maintained them. Some of the men stormed even the third line, and one was killed in one of the embrasures of that line.

I had reason to be satisfied with the conduct of the officers and troops during the siege of Burgos, particularly with the brigade of Guards.

The siege of Burgos was raised on the twenty-first: during the night the army filed under the walls of the castle, and crossed the bridge of the Arlanzon, which, although enfiladed by the artillery, was accomplished with scarcely any loss.

✶✶✶✶✶✶

The name of the French officer who commanded in Burgos was Colonel Le Breton. After the restoration of the Bourbons this officer held the rank of lieutenant-general, and whilst commanding in Strasburg, had an opportunity of paying military honours with that garrison to the Duke of Wellington, who was then on an inspection of the frontiers.

★★★★★★

By crossing this bridge, a march was gained on the enemy, who followed.

Reinforcements which had disembarked at Corunna, (Oct. 24th), under the Earl of Dalhousie, composed principally of the First Brigade of Guards, joined the army in position behind the Carrion. Next day the bridges over the Carrion and Pisuerga were blown up to arrest the progress of the enemy.

After the Allies left Cabeçon they destroyed the bridge, and crossed the Douro at Tudela and Puente del Duero. These bridges were also blown up; but in the evening the French passed in considerable force, by swimming the river near the bridge of Tordesillas. They then attacked and carried the ruins of the bridge, which was defended by a German battalion, and restored their communications.

Wellington, the next morning, moved to the left, and occupied nearly the same ground which the Allies had quitted previous to their former retreat on Salamanca. In this position the troops remained till the sixth November, when, they retired to Torrecilla del Ordem, and three days afterwards found themselves once more on the heights of St. Christoval, in front of Salamanca. Wellington broke up from the position and retired on Ciudad Rodrigo, which town he reached on the eighteenth. During the march from St. Christoval to Ciudad Rodrigo, the weather was extremely inclement, and the troops suffered severely from heavy roads, cold, and constant rain, which made it even difficult for them to light their fires; the supply of rations was also irregular.

The army crossed the Agueda, nineteenth and twentieth, and on the twenty-fourth of November headquarters were once more established at Freynada.

General Hill returned to Estramadura.

The troops went into cantonments for the winter. The Coldstream reached Musquetello on the sixth of December, where they were quartered.

	Officers present in the Peninsula	From	To		Officers absent.	Cause of absence.	From	To
Col.	Joseph Fuller	1 Jan.	31 May	M. Gl.	K. H. Howard, (2nd Major) }	Commanding a brigade	1 Jan.	31 Dec.
Lt.-Cl.	Hon. H. Brand	June	6 Oct.	,,	Richard Hulse	Ditto. Died	,,	7 Sept.
,,	James Philips	1 Jan.	Dec.	,,	H. Mac Kinnon	Ditto. Killed at Ciudad Rodrigo.	,,	19 Jan.
,,	Sir G. Stirling, Bart. }	,,	28 Feb.	,,	W. M. Peacocke	Commandant at Lisbon	,,	31 Dec.
,,	A. Woodford	,,	31 Dec.	Col.	Joseph Fuller	Posted to 2d Battn.	1 June	,,
Capt.	J. Macdonell	May	,,	,,	Matthew Lord Aylmer }	Asst. Adjutant Genl.Portugal }	1 Jan.	,,
	L. F. Adams, (Major) }	1 Jan.	April	Col.				
,,	W. H. Raikes	{ 1 Jan. / Aug. }	{ 26 Jan. / 31 Dec. }	Lt.-Cl.	Sir W. Sheridan	Prisoner of war	,,	,,
,,	Tho. Barrow	{ 1 Jan. / July }	{ 9 Feb. / 31 Dec. }	,,	Hon. H. Brand	Sick. In England	7 Oct.	,,
,,	Hon. W. Geo. Crofton }	1 Jan.	31 Dec.	,,	James Philips	Ordered to join 2d Battalion	Dec.	,,
,,	D. Mac Kinnon	June	Sept.			Retired by the		
,,	Hon. J. Walpole	1 Jan.	19 Nov.	,,	Sir G. Stirling	sale of his commission	1 Mar.	,,
,,	Thomas Steele	,,	31 Dec.					
,,	Edward Harvey	,,	18 Oct.			Qur. Mr. Genl.		
,,	W. Burroughs	July	31 Dec.	,,	R. D. Jackson	Dept. Portugal	1 Jan.	,,
,,	George Bowles	1 Jan.	,,					
,,	Thomas Sowerby	,,	,,	,,	H. F. Bouverie	Asst. Adjutant Genl.Portugal	,,	,,
,,	Ed. Lascelles, (appointed Adjut. vice Freemantle) }	April	,,	,,	Lucius F. Adams	To join 2d Battalion on promotion	April	,,
,,	P. Sandilands	,,	,,			Qr. Mr. Genl.	{ 1 Jan.	Feb.
,,	C. Mac Kenzie Fraser }	May	5 Oct.	Capt.	John Hamilton	Dept. Leave to Engd	{ Mar.	31 Dec.
Ens.	Charles White	1 Jan.	April			Sick leave in		
,,	Thomas Bligh	,,	,,			England.		
,,	Charles Shawe	,,	3 June	,,	Sir H. Sullivan	Posted to 2d Battalion	Jan.	31 Dec.
,,	George H. M. Greville }	,,	1 Nov.	,,	F. Miles Milman	Prisoner of war	1 ,,	,,
,,	John Talbot	,,	Dec.	,,	W. H. Raikes	Sick. Leave to England	27 ,,	Aug.
,,	G. H. Percival	,,	31 ,,	,,	Thomas Barrow	Leave to England	10 Feb.	July
,,	W. Geo. Baynes	,,	,,	,,	W. C. Wynyard	Adjt. Genl. Dept. Cadiz	1 Jan.	31 Dec.
,,	John S. Cowell	,,	,,			In England	{ 1 Jan.	May
,,	W. N. Burgess	,,	18 Oct.	,,	D. Mac Kinnon	Ditto. Sent recruiting	{ Sept.	31 Dec.
,,	John Mills	,,	31 Dec.			Sick, wounded.		
,,	James Bradshaw	,,	28 Oct.	,,	Hon. J. Walpole	Leave to England	20 Nov.	,,
,,	F. L. Beckford	,,	3 Oct.			land		
,,	J. C. Buckeridge	May	7 Oct.	,,	Henry Dawkins	Brigade Major, Portugal	1 Jan.	,,
,,	J. L. Blackman	April	31 Dec.					
,,	Will. Grimsted	,,	3 Oct.	,,	Edward Harvey	Killed before Burgos	18 Oct.	,,
,,	Beaumont Ld. Hotham }	{ April / 30 Nr. }	{ 22 July / 31 Dec. }	,,	John Freemantle	A. D. C. to the Marquis of Wellington	Nov.	,,
,,	Hon. John Rous	July	31 Dec.			Sick, wounded.		
,,	W. Anstruther	June	,,	,,	C. M. Fraser	Leave to England.	6 Oct.	,,
,,	Charles Shirley	Dec.	,,			land.		
,,	Fred. Vachell	1 Jan.	,,	,,	Charles White	To join 2d Bat. on promotion	April	,,
Adjut.	J. Freemantle, (Capt.) }	,,	Nov.					
Qu.Mr	John Holmes	,,	8 May					
Ast. Sur. }	Thomas Rose	,,	5 Oct.					

	Officers present in the Peninsula.	From	To		Officers absent.	Cause of absence.	From	To
As². Sur. }	Edward Nixon	1 Jan.	3 Dec.	Capt.	Thomas Bligh	{ To join 2d Bat. on promotion }	April	31 Dec.
,,	Thomas Maynard	Oct.	31 ,,	,,	Charles Shawe	Ditto.	4 June	,,
				,,	G. H. M. Greville	Ditto.	2 Nov.	,,
				,,	John Talbot	Ditto.	Dec.	,,
Qu.M'	Tho. Dwelly, (date of appointment) }	15 Oct.	27 ,,	Ens.	William Stothert	Prisoner of war	1 Jan.	,,
				,,	W. N. Burgess	{ Killed before Burgos	18 Oct.	,,
				,,	James Bradshaw	{ Leave. Joined 2d Battalion	29 Oct.	,,
				,,	F. L. Beckford	{ Sick leave. In England	4 Oct.	,,
				,,	J. C. Buckeridge	{ Killed before Burgos	7 Oct.	,,
				,,	Will. Grimsted	Leave to England	4 Oct.	,,
				,,	Beaumont Ld. Hotham }	{ Sick absent, wounded }	23 July	29 Nov.
				Qu.M'	John Holmes	{ To join 2d Bat. in England }	9 May	31 Dec.
				Bat. Sur. }	Charles Coombe	{ Sick absent. To England }	{ 1 Jan- Feb.	Feb. 31 Dec.
				As¹ Sur. }	Thomas Rose	Leave to England	6 Oct.	31 Dec.
				,,	Edward Nixon	Ditto.	4 Dec.	,,
				Qu.M'	Thomas Dwelly	{ To join 2d Bat. in England }	28 ,,	,,

CHAPTER 10

Battle of Vittoria

The loss sustained by Napoleon in Russia caused the defection of Prussia. The Crown Prince of Sweden called on the Germans to aid in the great work of restoring liberty to Europe. After the negotiations at Prague, Austria united with Russia, and Bavaria followed the example. The Russians advanced to the Elbe, and forced the French troops to retreat before them. The hostility of their former allies made the French suspicious of those that remained; and Napoleon thought it prudent to concentrate, that his communication with France might not be interrupted.

Soult, with a considerable portion of his troops, had been ordered to join the grand army in Germany: but notwithstanding this diminution, the force left in Spain amounted to upwards of one hundred and fifty thousand men; part of whom were in Catalonia and Valencia, the remainder spread over Castille, Leon, and the northern provinces.

All the requisite preparations for opening the campaign being completed, on the sixteenth of May five divisions under Graham crossed the Douro in boats, with orders to march on Zamora. Wellington, with the cavalry under General Fane, and a corps of Spaniards, reached Salamanca towards the end of the month. Sir Rowland Hill also arrived there from Estramadura.

The divisions under Graham first came up with the enemy on the Esla, who offered no opposition, but retired, destroying the bridges of Zamora and Toro. Pontoons were laid down and formed a bridge, over which the Allies crossed, and halted near Zamora. The French who occupied Madrid, and those on the Tagus, passed the Douro. Valladolid was evacuated, and the enemy retired to Burgos, a strong post.

After a reconnaissance under Sir Rowland Hill, General Reille was dislodged from the heights of Hormaza. The French Army retired on

Vittoria during the night of the twelfth of June, after having blown up about four hundred of their men in destroying the castle of Burgos. The Allies then moved to the left and crossed the Ebro near its source by the bridges of St. Martin and Fuentes de Arenas. On the eighteenth the light division was successful against a body of infantry. The enemy at Osma made a sharp attack on the first and fifth divisions under Graham, and although much superior in numbers, were repulsed and followed to Espejo. In this affair four men of the Coldstream were wounded.

In the night of the twelfth, the French, commanded by King Joseph, Marshal Jourdan acting as his major-general, concentrated in front of Vittoria; their right was stationed near that town, and extended across the Zadora on high ground covered by fieldworks; their left ran behind the river to the village of Subijana d'Alava, with an advance-post resting on the height in front, which terminated at Puebla d'Arlanzon; and the centre occupied a hill commanding the valley of Zadora, In this position their right covered the road from Bilboa, their left that from Logrono, and their centre the great road from Madrid.

Wellington reconnoitred the enemy's position on the twentieth. Next morning, he advanced in three corps; the right, composed of the second division, with a division of Portuguese under the Conde de Amarante, and Morillo's Spanish corps, commanded by Hill. The centre consisted of the fourth and light divisions. The left, comprising the first and fifth divisions with a body of cavalry, was under Graham. To this force was attached a division of Spaniards, who were ordered to make a wide movement, cross the Zadora, and enter the great road from Valladolid to Bayonne, and intercept the enemy in their retreat.

The right of the Allies first engaged above Puebla, and drove the enemy from the heights: reinforcements were sent from both sides; and after some severe fighting the hill was taken, retaken, and taken again; when it remained in possession of General Hill's corps, who followed up his success. The centre divisions passed the Zadora over some bridges intended for foot-passengers, Picton's and the seventh division crossed the bridge on the Mendonza road, and drove the enemy before them, with the loss of twenty-eight guns. The French retired in good order on Vittoria.

Graham, whose column on the previous evening had been sent to Margiana, advanced by the road from Bilboa to Vittoria: he attacked the front and flank of the right, and succeeded in driving the French from their position above Abechuco. Every exertion was then made by the enemy to regain Gamorra-Major; and although they failed,

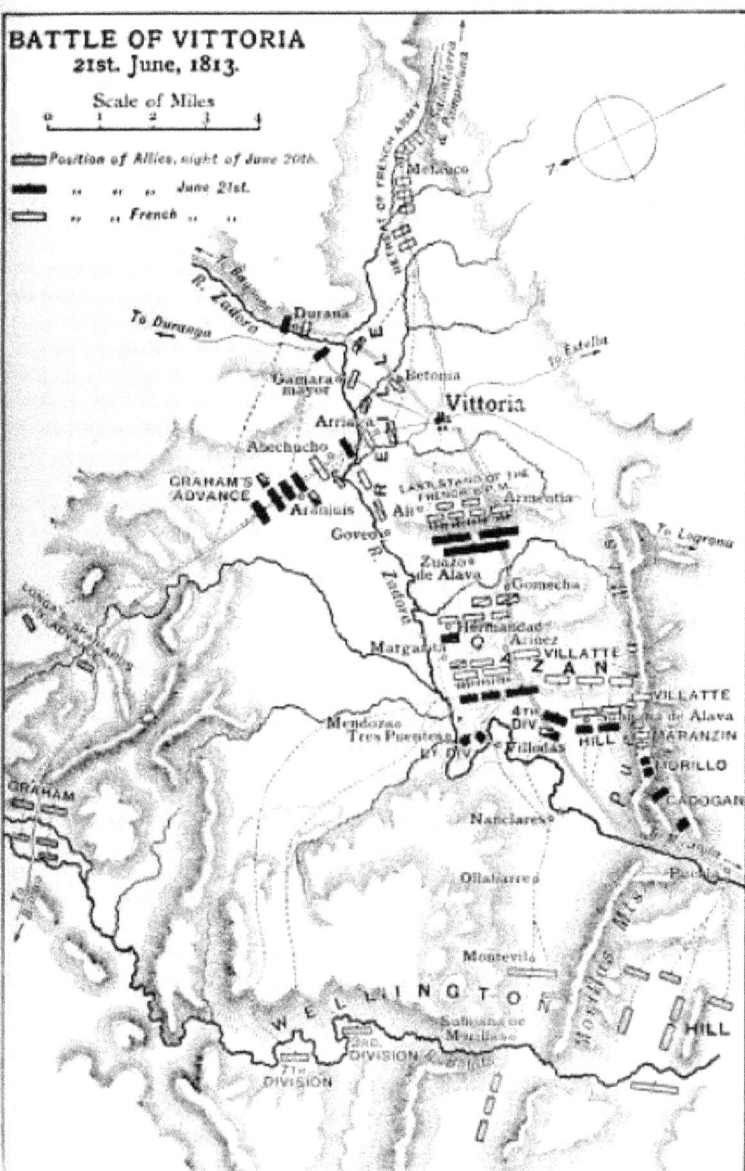

BATTLE OF VITTORIA
21st. June, 1813.

Scale of Miles

0   1   2   3   4

▬▬▬ *Position of Allies, night of June 20th.*

▬▬▬ " " " June 21st.

▭▭▭ " " " French " "

R. Bayas

R. Zadorra

To Duranga →

Durana

Gamara mayor

Betona

Arriaga

Abechucho

Vittoria

GRAHAM'S ADVANCE

Aranuis

Ali

Armentia

Gobeo

LAST STAND OF THE FRENCH 6 P.M.

Zuazo de Alava

Gomecha

To Logrono

Margarita

Hermandad Arinez

Mendozae

Tres Puentes

4th DIV

Lt DIV

Gillodas

VILLATTE

ZAN

VILLATTE

Subij. de Alava

MARANZIN

MORILLO

HILL

CADOGAN

Nanclares

Ollabarres

Montevito

GRAHAM

Subijana de Morillas

W E L L I N G T O N

2nd DIVISION

7th DIVISION

P U E B L A M T S.

H I L L

RETREAT OF FRENCH ARMY

To Salvatierra & Pampeluna

Metauco

R. Estela

To Estella

they prevented General Oswald's division from profiting by the advantage first gained. The entrance of the centre division into Vittoria obliged the enemy to retire, that they might avoid being taken in rear. The division then crossed the river and posted themselves on the high road to Bayonne, driving back the French on the road leading to Pampeluna, the only one left open to them.

Confusion and dismay spread among the enemy's ranks, who were pressed on all sides; and had it not been for the local impediments which opposed the progress of the artillery and cavalry, the French army would have been annihilated. One hundred and fifty-one guns were taken, besides vast quantities of ammunition, caissons, and baggage, together with Marshal Jourdan's *bâton*. The loss of the enemy is pretended by their own historians not to have exceeded six thousand men: that of the Allies was under five thousand.

After this battle the left, under Graham, advanced on Bilboa, in hopes of intercepting General Foy, who on receiving the account of Joseph's defeat retired on Bayonne. At Tolosa he made a stand; but Graham attacked and drove him beyond the frontier. The left wing kept advancing towards Bayonne, forcing the enemy from every position where they attempted any resistance.

At this period colour-sergeants were first introduced, in the proportion of one to each company.

★★★★★★

War-Office, 27th July, 1813.

Sir,—I have the honour to acquaint you, that in consideration of the meritorious services of the non-commissioned officers of the army, and with the view of extending encouragements and advantages to those ranks of the infantry, corresponding to the benefits which the appointment of troop sergeant-major offers in the cavalry; His Royal Highness the Prince Regent has been most graciously pleased, in the name and on the behalf of His Majesty, to order, that from the 25th June, 1813, inclusive, the pay of the sergeant-major in every regiment of infantry not subject to a limitation of service as to place, shall be increased to three shillings *per diem*.

His Royal Highness has also been pleased to order, that from the same date, one sergeant of the establishment in each company of the said regiments shall be designated "Colour-Sergeant," and that his pay shall be raised to two shillings and four-pence *per diem*.

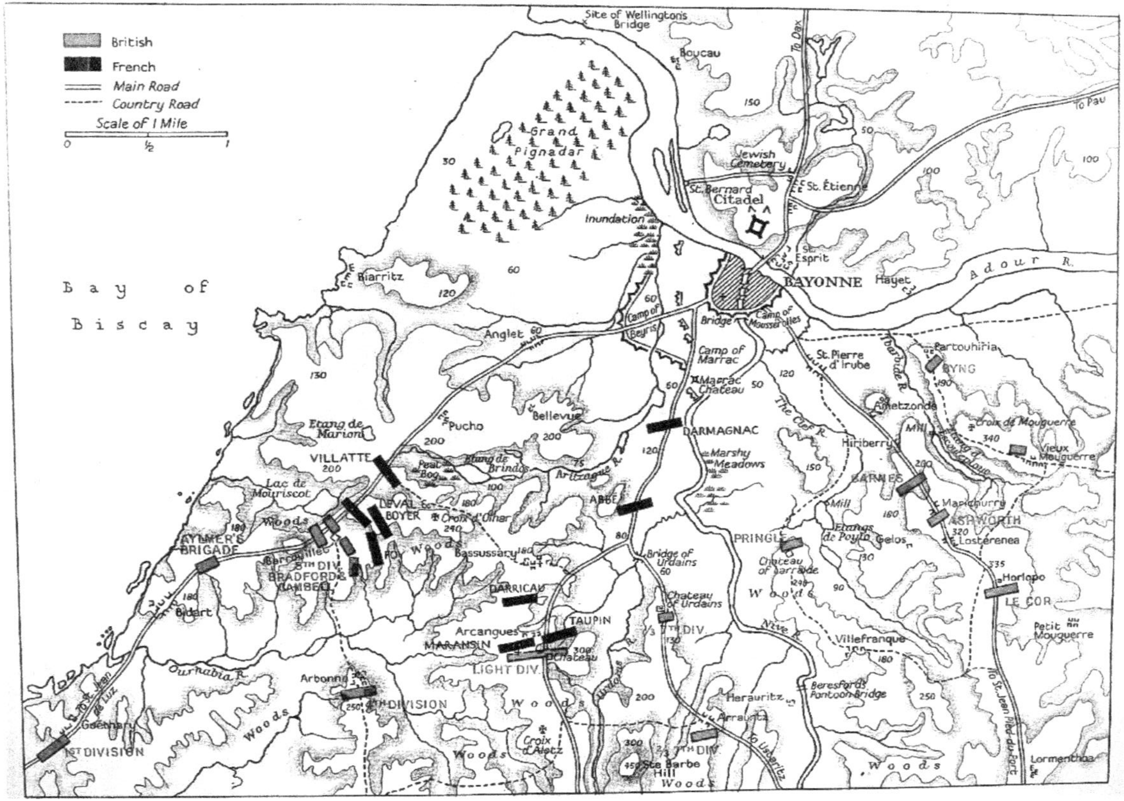
British
French
Main Road
Country Road
Scale of 1 Mile
0
½
1
Bay of Biscay
Site of Wellington's Bridge
Boucau
To Dax
To Pau
Grand Pignadar
Jewish Cemetery
St. Bernard
Citadel
St. Étienne
St. Esprit
BAYONNE
Hayet
Adour R.
Inundation
Biarritz
Anglet
Camp of Beyris
Bridge
Camp of Mousserolles
Camp of Marrac
Marrac Chateau
St. Pierre d'Irube
Partouhiria
BYNG
Croix de Mouguerre
Vieux Mouguerre
Ametzonde
Etang de Marion
Pucho
Bellevue
DARMAGNAC
Marshy Meadows
The Cor R.
Hiriberry
Mill
BARNES
Maritchurry
ASHWORTH
Losterenea
Horlopo
LE COR
Petit Mouguerre
VILLATTE
Peat Bog
Etang de Brindos
Arritzague R.
Lac de Mouriscot
LEVAL
BOYER
Croix d'Oihar
ABBÉ
Woods
AYLMER'S BRIGADE
Barouillet
5TH DIV
BRADFORD
HAMBER
FOY
Bassussary
Bridge of Urdains
PRINGLE
Chateau of Barrade
Etangs de Poyto
Gelos
DARRICAU
Chateau of Urdains
7TH DIV
TAUPIN
Arcangues
MARANSIN
Chateau
LIGHT DIV
Bidart
Villefranque
Nive R.
Ourhabia R.
Arbonne
6TH DIVISION
Herauritz
Beresford's Pontoon Bridge
Arrauntz
To Ustaritz
To St. Jean Pied-du-Port
Croix d'Alotz
Ste Barbe Hill
Guéthary
To St. Jean de Luz
1ST DIVISION
Lormenthoa

The colour-sergeants are to be distinguished by an honourable badge; of which, however, and of the advantages attending it, they will, in case of misconduct, be liable to be deprived, at the discretion of the colonel or commanding-officer of the regiment, or by the sentence of a court-martial. It is also intended, that the duty of attending the colours in the field shall at all times be performed by the colour-sergeant; but that these distinctions shall not be permitted to interface with the regular performance of their regimental and company duties.

I have the honour to be. Sir, &c.

Colonel of the . . . regiment of Foot.   Palmerston.

Mem.—The pay of the sergeant-major in each battalion of Foot Guards was increased, from the period above mentioned, by the nett addition of 6*d*, *per diem*, making his nett pay 3*s*. 2*d*. *per diem*; and the pay of the colour-sergeant per company in those battalions was also augmented by the same additional rate, making his nett pay 2*s*. 6*d*. *per diem* in all."

On the 24th of July, 1814, a circular letter was written, directed to the general officers of the Foot Guards, by command of His Royal Highness the Duke of York, and signed by the Military Secretary, notifying His Royal Highnesses intention to remove them from their regimental commissions. Field officers and captains of the Guards, who were general officers, and "in the enjoyment of advantages peculiar to that branch of the service," were to receive as a compensation an increased rate of pay.

★★★★★★

July 1st, Wellington decided on besieging St. Sebastian; a desirable point for establishing the communication with England. Sir Thomas Graham invested that place with the first and fifth divisions. To save time batteries were erected on the sand-hills. The convent of St. Bartholomew was carried on the seventeenth. Two breaches were deemed practicable on the twenty-fifth. A mine sprung under the glacis of the front line was the signal for a party of two thousand men, who were in readiness at daybreak, to rush forward.

This unexpected explosion created so much alarm, that it enabled the assailants to reach the breach with little loss; but in their attempt to ascend they were checked by a front and flank fire, which destroyed five hundred; when the remainder fell back on their trenches. The same day the garrison made a sortie, and succeeded in taking many Portuguese prisoners.

Soult returned from Germany to command the French force in the south. His first object was to relieve Pampeluna, which had been invested by a corps of Spaniards; after various conflicts, he advanced in two columns, amounting to thirty-five thousand men, against the passes of Roncesvalles and Maya, near the mountain Cubiry. He was, however, repulsed in his attacks, and retreated with his army early on the thirty-first, in three columns, by St Jean Pied de Port, Echalar, Sarré, and Maya. The Allied Army followed and came up with the enemy's rear-guard, strongly posted in the pass of Donna Maria, from whence they were driven by the brigade under General Barnes.

The loss of the French since Soult had resumed the command was upwards of eight thousand men, and greatly exceeded that of the Allies.

Lord Wellington in the beginning of August returned to the position occupied by his army previous to the advance of Soult.

Supplies of stores and a battering train arrived from England, and were landed on the eighteenth of August,

Towards the end of the month, (28th), the Allies had placed nearly eighty guns in battery before St. Sebastian, whose fire on the town continued without intermission during the day from their first opening. On the night of the twenty-ninth the garrison attempted another sortie, and were repulsed.

The storming party, which formed early on the thirty-first, consisted of seven hundred and fifty volunteers, two hundred of whom were supplied by the Guards. The detachment from the Coldstream consisted of one lieutenant, one ensign, two sergeants, one drummer, and fifty men, under Captain Barrow and Ensign Chaplin.

The column, after many desperate attempts, found itself, on reaching the summit, assailed by a heavy fire from the place, that destroyed all in the advance. In the words of General Graham:

No man outlived the attempt to gain the ridge.
Notwithstanding the great extent of the breach, there was but one point where it was possible to enter, and there by files. All the inside of the wall to the right of the curtain formed a perpendicular scarp of at least twenty feet to the level of the streets, so that the narrow ridge of the curtain itself, formed by the breaching of its end and front, was the only accessible points. During the suspension of the operations of the siege, the enemy had prepared every means of defence which art could devise.

It was not till the attack renewed, and after a most determined assault, that the besieged were driven from their defences. The Allies then succeeded in forcing the barricades, and pushed forward into the town, with a loss of about two thousand three hundred killed and wounded. The enemy retired to the castle, leading about seven hundred prisoners.

The casualties in the Coldstream were, five rank and file killed. Ensign Thomas Chaplin and twenty-seven rank and file wounded, and one missing.

On the ninth of September, fifty heavy guns and mortars opened on the castle of St. Sebastian; which, after a bombardment of two hours, surrendered. The garrison amounted to upwards of two thousand, including about five hundred sick.

On the seventh of October, the first and fifth divisions, with General Wilson's Portuguese brigade, forded the Bidassoa at low water, for the purpose of driving the enemy from the mountain of La Rhune. A corps of Spaniards crossed the river higher up, with the intention of attacking the works on the Montagne Vert. General Alten with the light division, and the Spaniards under Longa, were to attack the pass of Bera. General Giron with the Army of Andalusia was to march against the entrenchments of La Rhune, The fifth division crossed the river, followed by the first, and advanced against the French, who had scarcely formed in line before they were driven from their works, with the loss of several guns.

At Bern the attack of the light division was particularly successful. General Giron carried the lower slopes of La Rhune; the enemy, however, crowned the heights, when the close of day put an end to further efforts.

Next day the Spaniards carried an intrenched line beyond the mountain with little opposition. These advantages were gained with a loss of about sixteen hundred men. In the Coldstream the casualties were, two rank and file killed and ten wounded.

On the eighteenth the Coldstream moved to the camp near St. Jean de Luz.

On the thirty-first, after a blockade of four months, the garrison of Pampeluna surrendered prisoners of war.

The enemy from the beginning of August had been in possession of a formidable line of works on the Nivelle; their right rested on the sea, covered the town of St, Jean de Luz, and extended twelve miles in a direct line; their centre occupied the village of Sarré and the adjacent rising ground; their left, covered by the River Ainhoe, rested on a height, which was defended by several works that added to the strength of their position. A mountain protected the approach to the village, the extremity of which was also fortified. In the progress of these works no labour or expense had been spared.

The incessant rain and snow in the mountains greatly retarded Lord Wellington.

On crossing the Bidassoa, Graham, who had been appointed to head the force in Holland, was succeeded in command of the left wing of the army by Sir John Hope. It consisted of the first division under Major-General Howard, with the fifth division, the independent, and two Portuguese brigades. The centre was formed in two columns, the right of which comprised the thirds fourth, and seventh divisions under Marshal Beresford; and the left, the light division, with the Spanish Army of reserve, supported by a brigade of cavalry. The sixth and Portuguese division under Sir John Hamilton, and the Spanish division commanded by Morillo, formed the right wing.

In Germany the French lost their character for invincibility and were deserted by their auxiliaries: the results of which were apparent in the subsequent victories of the Confederates and the ultimate downfall of Napoleon's power. He could no longer send reinforcements to recover the ground lost in Spain; and Wellington resolved to pass into France.

Previous to entering that country, the British commander issued the following humane and generous proclamation:

Officers and soldiers must recollect, that their nations are at war with France, solely because the ruler of the French nation will not allow them to be at peace, and is desirous of forcing them to submit to his yoke; and they must not forget, that the worst of the evils suffered by the enemy, in his profligate invasion of Spain and Portugal, have been occasioned by the irregularities of his soldiers, and their cruelties, authorised and encouraged by their chiefs, toward the unfortunate and peaceful inhabitants of the country. To avenge this conduct on the peaceable inhabitants of France, would be unmanly and unworthy of the nations to which the Commander of the Forces now addresses himself.

Calm and confident, Wellington, from the heights of the Pyrenees, looked down on the well-guarded territories of the great enemy of his country, and, with steady purpose, prepared to tame the pride of a mighty prince who, while he carried war and misery into almost every capital of Europe, made it his haughty boast that the women of the great nation had never seen the smoke of an enemy's camp. The Herculean task of the British general was accomplished; he had chased the far-famed legions of Napoleon from the gates of Lisbon to the utmost limits of the Spanish boundary, and had restored the affrighted inhabitants of the Peninsula to their native towns and villages in peace and safety. His was no selfish triumph, destined only to convey to future ages the name of a successful conqueror.

Wellington stood before the world at once a hero and a benefactor; and the shouts of his exulting soldiers were mingled with the blessings of rescued millions, whom his genius and courage had delivered from the grasp of the oppressor. It was his high and peculiar glory that the brilliant achievements in Spain and Portugal, which secured him an imperishable reputation as a commander, gave repose to unoffending nations, and had no object but to foil a military chief whose restless unscrupulous ambition rendered murder, conflagration, and pillage familiar to the sight of every neighbouring kingdom that dared to resist his usurpations. After long and carefully perusing the living map that lay spread out beneath his feet, Wellington ordered his army to advance; and on the tenth of November the troops descended from the Pyrenees through the mountain passes by moonlight, to transfer to France the calamities of domestic war, and teach the admirers of splendid but unprincipled aggression, that there is at length a day of retribution.

The Allies on reaching the line of piquets halted, preparatory to the attack, which was to commence at daylight; they were so placed as to be concealed from the enemy.

At the dawn of day, a cannonade was commenced against some redoubts in front of Sarré, after which the infantry rushed to the assault and carried the works and the village. The light division forced the lines on Petite la Rhune. The enemy having abandoned the redoubts. General Alten formed on the summit of the hill they had quitted. The army then advanced, covered by skirmishers towards the heights behind Sarré, when the French successively abandoned their entrenchments, and fled in great disorder, (Nov. 10th), down the hill with a view to reach the bridges over the Nivelle.

Whilst the light division was proceeding to assault a redoubt, the garrison endeavoured to escape; Beresford, however, intercepted them and made about six hundred prisoners.

Clinton received orders to ford the Nivelle, and attack the heights of Ainhoe, supported by General Hamilton's division placed in *échelon*. He marched directly on the right to attack the enemy in front, who, being driven back, left the redoubts on the heights of Ainhoe unprotected. The French detachments by which they were occupied hastily retreated, and caused a body of their troops on the left to recede. The British divisions then advanced, when the French quitted the line in front of Ainhoe and retired towards Cambo.

The enemy, driven from the centre of their line, concentrated on the heights above St. Pé whence they were dislodged whilst forming, by a flank movement of the third and seventh divisions on the left, in conjunction with the sixth division which marched in the opposite direction. The centre of the Allies was established in rear of the enemy's right. The close of day put an end to the operations, and Soult, under cover of the night, withdrew, and retired to Bayonne.

During these movements the enemy lost fifty guns, two thousand men, fifteen hundred prisoners, and great quantities of stores and ammunition.

The loss of the Allies was under six hundred killed, two thousand wounded. Ensign Anstruther and thirteen rank and file of the light company of the Coldstream were wounded.

The Allies went into cantonments between the ridge of Nivelle and the sea. Soult concentrated his army in an entrenched camp in front of Bayonne.

The distance between the contending armies did not exceed two miles at the nearest point, which induced Wellington to construct a defensive line for the protection of his front against any sudden attack.

The Coldstream advanced on the ninth December, beyond Bidart, within three miles of Bayonne, encountered the enemy, and returned at night to their quarters at St. Jean de Luz (Headquarters.)

The allied army advanced on the ninth of December, and the left wing, under Hope, closely reconnoitred the enemy's intrenchments at Bayonne, with little opposition. Hill passed the Nive by the fords at Cambo. Clinton's division crossed by the bridge of boats at Ustariz.

The French made a stand at Ville Franque; but were dislodged by the light infantry of Clinton's division. In the night the enemy withdrew all their posts into the town of Bayonne.

Next day Hill's corps took post with their right on the Adour, the left reaching to Ville Franque, and their centre across the road from Bayonne to St. Jean Pied de Port; some cavalry were also sent to Urcuray to watch a division of the enemy posted near St. Palais. Sir John Hope

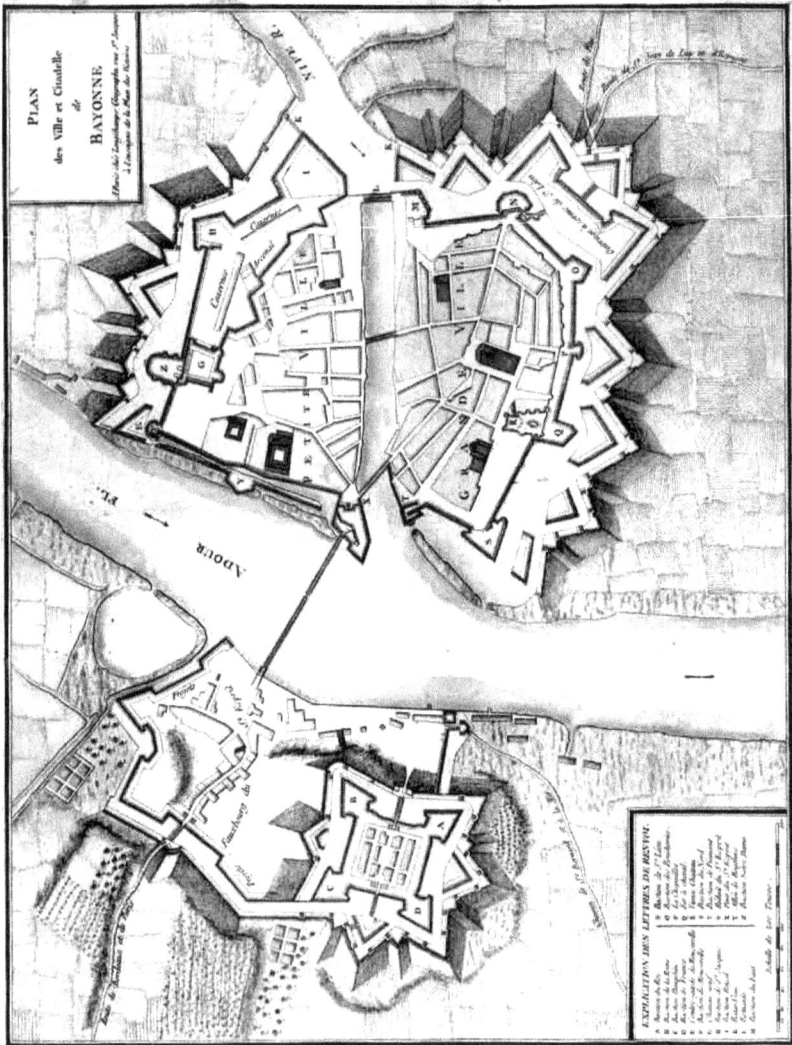

PLAN
des Ville et Citadelle
de
BAYONNE.

returned to his former cantonment, and Beresford retired to the left bank of the Nive, keeping up his communication with General Hill by a bridge of boats. Soult left Bayonne early on the morning of the tenths and advanced with the determination of attacking the left under Hope.

The road to St. Jean de Luz was defended by the fifth division and two Portuguese brigades. The light division was placed about two miles to the right, and separated from the left corps by a range of hills, too steep to tenable a body of troops to occupy them.

The French attacked and drove the light division within the village of Arcanques, where they were strongly entrenched, and afterwards established themselves on the hills. This being effected, the enemy attacked the left, consisting of the fifth division, which received them with great gallantry: General Robinson was wounded; and the French having advanced in front of Barouillet through some wood, compelled Major-General Campbell's Portuguese brigade, and General Robinson's brigade which supported it, to retire, and thereby they forced the position.

A Portuguese battalion moved forward on the road, and went into the rear of the wood: the Ninth regiment on the extreme right wheeled round and charged with the Portuguese, by which the enemy were driven back and suffered severely. The French, however, again renewed the attempt to dislodge the fifth division, when the remainder of the left wing, consisting of the brigade of Guards, brought up from their cantonments under Major-General Howard, opportunely arrived: the enemy's attacking columns were then repulsed; and night closed on the combatants.

Soult, having failed in his efforts to destroy the left of the Allies, retired with part of his force during the night from the position in front of Sir John Hope. This general next day sent some of his troops to the support of the light division; and being thus weakened, he was again attacked by the enemy, whom he repulsed. On the same day the Coldstream moved to the outposts, whence they afterwards returned to their quarters at St. Jean de Lux; but were occasionally sent to the outpost near Bidart.

The French still continued in front of the left, and on the afternoon of the twelfth there was some sharp skirmishing, (the Coldstream had three men wounded), but no alteration took place in the position of either army. Little else of interest occurred pending these operations, with the exception of some unsuccessful attacks made by Soult on the corps of Sir Rowland Hill, which commenced on the ninth and ended on the thirteenth of December. Although Soult from his position was enabled to direct his whole force against any given point of the extended line of the Allies with a great superiority in numbers, yet he made no impression by these attacks. The loss of life on both sides was, however, considerable.

RETURN OF THE OFFICERS OF THE FIRST BATTALION OF THE COLDSTREAM FOR THE YEAR 1813.

Officers present in the Peninsula.	From	To	Officers absent.	Cause of absence.	From	To
Lt.Cl. A. Woodford	1 Jan.	31 Dec.				
,, J. Macdonell	,,	,,				
,, G. Collier	Jan.	,,				
,, J. Hamilton	. July	,,				
Capt. W. H. Raikes	1 Jun.	16 May				
,, Thomas Gore	March	31 Dec.				
,, T. Barrow, (Major)	1 Jan.	22 ,,				
,, Hon. W. G. Crofton	,,	31 ,,				
,, Thomas Steele	,,	,,				
,, W. Burroughs	,,	,,				
,, G. Bowles	,,	,,				
,, T. Sowerby	,,	,,				
,, P. Sandilands	,,	,,				
,, John Prince	. Jan.	,,				
,, J. V. Harvey	July	,,				
Ens. G. H. Perceval	1 Jan.	14 Mar.				
,, W. G. Baynes	,,	21 July				
,, J. S. Cowell	,,	Oct.				
,, John Mills	,,	Jun.				
,, J. L. Blackman	,,	31 Dec.				
,, B. Lord Hotham	,,	,,				
,, Hon. J. Rous	,,	,,				
,, W. Anstruther	,,	,,				
,, C. Shirley	,,	,,				
,, J. Drummond	. Jan.	,,				
,, Hon. R. Moore	. ,,	,,				
,, C. A. Girardot	. ,,	,,				
,, T. Chaplin	May	26 Sept.				
,, E. Clifton	July	31 Dec.				
,, Henry Salwey	Sept.	,,				
,, G. G. Morgan	,,	,,				
,, F. Vachell	1 Jan.	,,				
,, W. Kortright	. ,,	,,				
Adjt. F. Lascelles, (Capt.)	1 ,,	,,				
Q.Mr. B. Selway	. ,,	,,				
Surg. Thomas Rose	July	,,				
Ast. Sur. W. Whymper	June	,,				
,, T. Maynard	1 Jan.	,,				
			Lt.-G. J. Calcraft, 1st Major	Leave	1 Jan.	31 Dec.
			M.-G. K. A. Howard, 2d Maj.	Commanding a Brigade	,,	,,
			,, W. M. Peacocke	Commandant at Lisbon	,,	,,
			,, M. Lord Aylmer	Ast.Adjt.Gen. Portugal / Commanding a Brigade	Jan. / July	June / 31 Dec.
			Lt.Cl. Sir W. Sheridan	Prisoner of war	1 Jan.	,,
			,, Hon. H. Brand	In England. Posted to 2d battalion	,,	,,
			,, R. D. Jackson	Asst. Q.-Mr. Gl. Portugal / Leave to Engd / Returned	1 Jan. / Oct.	April / 31 Dec.
			,, H. F. Bouverie	Ast Adjt.Gen. Peninsula	1 Jan.	,,
			,, W. H. Raikes	Sick leave to England / Posted to 2d battalion	18 May / July	June / 31 Dec.
			Major T. Barrow	Leave to England	23 Dec.	,,
			Capt. W. C. Wynyard	Adjut. Gen. Dept. Cadiz / On Staff at home	1 Jan. / Aug.	July / 31 Dec.
			,, Hon. J. Walpole	Sick, wounded, England / OnStaff, Kent district	1 Jan.	,,
			,, H. Dawkins	Brig.-Major, Sec. Brigade of Guards	,,	,,
			,, J. Freemantle	A. D. C. to Marquis of Wellington	,,	,,
			,, A. Wedderburn	A. D. C. to Lt.-Gen. Sir John Hope	,,	,,
			,, W. G. Baynes	To England on promotion	22 July	,,
			,, J. S. Cowell	To England on promotion	Oct.	,,
			Ens. G. H. Perceval	To join 2d batt.	15 Mar.	,,
			,, W. Stothert	Prisoner of war	1 Jan.	,,
			,, John Mills	Leave to England	Feb.	,,
			,, F. L. Beckford	Sick, England Recruiting	1 Jan.	,,
			,, W. Grimstead	Leave in England.	,,	,,
			,, T. Chaplin	Sick, wounded: to England	27 Sept.	,,

CHAPTER 11

Coldstream Suffer Severely

The severity of the season obliged the Allies to keep in their cantonments, and consequently nothing of moment occurred until about the middle of February, 1814, when Wellington endeavoured to draw Soult from his position near Bayonne.

On the fourteenth of February Hill's corps broke up in Urcuray and moved to Hellete, from whence they obliged the enemy's troops to retire on St. Palais, General Harispe left a garrison at St. Jean Pied de Port, which was blockaded by the Spanish corps under Mina, and, being joined by other troops, made a stand on the height of La Montagne, whence he was driven, and crossed the Bidassoa. The left wing of the Allies, intended for the investment of Bayonne, moved forward at one o'clock a.m. on the morning of the twenty-third, driving the enemy's outposts before them: the heavy guns were then brought up and placed in battery.

The River Adour was to be crossed by means of pontoon rafts, which could only be worked during slack tide. In the evening, when two light companies of the Coldstream and Third Guards, with four battalion companies of the latter regiment, had passed, two columns of the enemy deployed, fired a volley, and rushed on them with the bayonet. The Guards, however, being most judiciously posted by Major-General Stopford on a ridge of sand, with their right resting on the river, their left towards the sea, the allied artillery on the other side flanking the ground in their front, and assisted by a discharge of Congreve rockets, threw the enemy into confusion and forced them to retire. (See *The Details of the Rocket System* by William Congreve; Leonaur, 2020.)

In the night pontoons, used as row-boats, were substituted for the rafts; and, as only fifteen men passed over each turn, it was not until the evening of the next day that the first division and some cavalry were on the right bank. By the twenty-sixth a bridge was constructed below the town, which during the remainder of the war served as the regular communication between St. Jean de Luz and Spain. The following evening, after a sharp skirmish, Bayonne was blockaded. Sir John Hope with the left wing was intrusted with the siege. The direct road to Bourdeaux was now open by the bridge thrown across the Adour.

Wellington on the twenty-seventh of February attacked Soult, whose army, strongly posted near Orthez, had successfully resisted the repeated efforts of the Allies to gain the heights. But the British commander determined to change his plan; the result was the brilliant, rapid, and total defeat of the French, who sustained a loss of three thousand men and six pieces of artillery. The casualties on the part of the Allies did not exceed two thousand five hundred,

Soult retired towards Tarbes by the road to Toulouse: in consequence of the heavy rains and the destruction of the bridges the French were not closely pursued in their retreat.

Wellington had been informed that, although favourable to the Bourbon cause, the inhabitants of Bourdeaux were prevented from giving vent to their feelings by a small garrison which kept them in awe. Soult probably supposed that Wellington would not advance on this town while the garrison of Bayonne held out. Marshal Beresford, having with him the Duc d'Angoulême, was however ordered to march with his corps to expel the French troops from Bourdeaux; but they immediately retired on his approach, and the English general was met by the entire population, who instantly destroyed all the emblems of Napoleon. Wellington, considering that so large a force was unnecessary for the defence of Bourdeaux, recalled Beresford, leaving Lord Dalhousie there with about five thousand men.

On the tenth of April the Battle of Toulouse was gained, though not without great loss. The British and Portuguese had five thousand killed and wounded, and the Spaniards nearly three thousand; but, in estimating this fatal result, it must be remembered that the attack continued during the entire day, and was directed against intrenchments of a most formidable description. The loss of the French was three thousand six hundred.

Wellington closely pressed the siege of Toulouse, and on the night of the twelfth Soult retired, leaving three generals and one thousand six hundred prisoners.

Early on the morning of the fourteenth, and after the intelligence of the event which had occurred at Paris on the seventh was known, a desperate sortie was made from the French camp in front of the citadel of Bayonne, directed principally against the position occupied by the Second Brigade of Guards at St. Etienne, opposite to the citadel.

★★★★★★

On the eleventh of April, 1814, the treaty of Paris was ratified by Marshals Ney, Macdonald, and Caulaincourt, on the part of Napoleon; and by the Ministers of Austria, Russia, and Prussia. By the convention, Napoleon renounced all sovereignty over France and Italy; stipulating that the Island of Elba should be his domain and residence during life: the abdication was signed at Fontainebleau.

★★★★★★

Major-General Hay was killed at the first onset, and the enemy gained temporary possession of the village of St. Etienne. The centre of the British was also driven in, and General Stopford was wounded. General Hope, on coming up with some troops in the dark, encountered the enemy, by whom he was wounded and taken prisoner, his horse having been shot under him. Reinforcements were quickly brought up, the lost ground recovered, and the assailants driven back with great slaughter: but this was a lamentable and useless waste of lives, as Napoleon had already abdicated.

The Allies lost more than eight hundred men in killed, wounded, and prisoners.

The casualties of the Coldstream in consequence of this sortie from Bayonne were, one captain, one lieutenant, one sergeant, one drummer, and thirty rank and file killed; one captain, three lieutenants, two ensigns, eleven sergeants, and one hundred and eleven rank and file wounded; two sergeants and eighty-two rank and file missing. Lieutenant-Colonel Sir Henry Sullivan and Captain the Honourable W, G. Crofton were killed, Lieutenant-Colonel Collier, who died, having had both his thighs amputated; Captain Burroughs, Ensigns Vachell and Pitt died of their wounds. Captains James Vigoro Harvey and Henry Dawkins were wounded.

Thus, closed hostilities on land between two nations who had been engaged in an incessant warfare, with only one year's interruption, from 1793.

The Coldstream left their ground near Bayonne on the second of May: after being encamped some time they marched to Bourdeaux,

RETURN OF THE OFFICERS OF THE FIRST BATTALION OF THE COLDSTREAM FROM JANUARY TO JULY, 1814.

	Present.	From.	To
Lt.Cl.	A. Woodford	1 Jan.	July
,,	J. Macdonell	,,	31 Jan.
,,	George Collier	,,	10 May
,,	John Hamilton	,,	July
,,	Sir H. Sullivan, Bt.	March	14 Apr.
,,	Thomas Gore	1 Jan.	11 Feb.
Capt.	Hon. W. G. Crofton	,,	14 Apr.
,,	Thomas Steele	,,	July
,,	W. Burroughs	,,	26 Apr.
,,	George Bowles	,,	July
,,	Tho. Sowerby	,,	,,
,,	P. Sandilands	,,	,,
,,	John Prince	,,	9 Jan.
,,	J. V. Harvey	,,	June
Ens.	J. L. Blackman	,,	4 April
,,	Beaumont Ld. Hotham	,,	Feb.
,,	Hon. J. Rous	,,	May
,,	W. Anstruther	,,	13 Feb.
,,	Chas. Shirley	,,	8 June
,,	J. Drummond	,,	July
,,	Hon. R. Moore	,,	,,
,,	C. A. Girardot	,,	,,
,,	Edw. Clifton	,,	,,
,,	Henry Salwey	,,	
,,	G. G. Morgan	,,	,,
,,	Fred. Vachell	,,	13 May
,,	Hon. J. Forbes	March	July
,,	William Pitt	,,	24 Apr.
,,	Wm. Kortright	1 Jan.	July
,,	H. Armytage	March	,,
,,	Hon. Wm. Rufus Rous	,,	,,
,,	Henry J. W. Bentinck	April	,,
Adjut.	E. Lascelles, (Capt.)	1 Jan.	,,
Q.Mr.	Benj. Selway	,,	,,
Surg.	Thomas Rose	,,	June
Ast. Sur.	W. Whymper	,,	4 Jan.
,,	Thos. Maynard	,,	July

	Absent.	Cause of absence.	From	To
Lt.-G.	J. Calcraft, (1st Major)	Leave	1 Jan.	July
M.-G.	Harry Chester	Ditto	,,	,,
,,	Warren M. Peacocke	Commandant at Lisbon	,,	,,
,,	Joseph Fuller	Staff, at home	,,	,,
,,	Matth. Lord Aylmer	Coms. a Brigade in France	,,	,,
Lt.Cl.	Sir W. Sheridan	Prisoner of war	,,	—
,,	R. D. Jackson	Ast. Qur. Mr. Gl. in France	,,	,,
,,	H. F. Bouverie	Ast. Adjt. Gl. in France	,,	,,
,,	J. Macdonell	Ordered to join Detacht in Holland	1 Feb.	—
,,	George Collier	Died of his wounds	10 May	
,,	Sir H. Sullivan	Killed at Bayonne	14 Apr.	—
,,	Thomas Gore	To join 2d Bn. on prom.	12 Feb.	—
Capt.	Th. Barrow, (Maj.)	Leave in England	1 Jan.	July
,,	W. Clinton Wynyard	A.D.C. to Maj.Gl. Acland: died	,,	27 Apr.
,,	Hon. W. G. Crofton	Killed at Bayonne	14 Apr.	—
,,	D. MacKinnon	Recruiting in England	1 Jan.	July
,,	Hon. J. Walpole	Staff, at home	,,	,,
,,	Hen. Dawkins	Brig. Maj. to 2d brigade of Guards. Sick, wounded, to Engd.	,, / 9 June	8 June / July
,,	W. Burroughs	Died of his wounds	26 Apr.	—
,,	J. Freemantle, (Maj.)	A.D.C. to Marquis of Wellington	1 Jan.	July
,,	John Prince	Leave to England	10 ,,	,,
,,	Js. V. Harvey	Sick, wounded, to Engd.	June	,,
,,	A. Wedderburn	A.D.C. to Sir J. Hope	1 Jan.	,,
,,	Charles White	A.D.C. to the Duke of Cambridge	,, ,,	,,
,,	W. Stothert	Prisoner of war	,, ,,	—
,,	J. L. Blackman	To join 2d Bn. on prom.	5 Apr.	,,
,,	Beaumont Ld. Hotham	Ditto do.	Feb.	,,
,,	W. Anstruther	Sick, wounded, to Engd.	14 ,,	,,
,,	Hon. J. Rous	To join 2d Bn. on prom.	June	,,
,,	Charles Shirley	Ditto do.	9 June	,,
Ens.	Fred. Vachell	Died of his wounds	13 May	—
,,	Hon. J. Forbes	With 2d battalion	1 Jan.	Feb.
,,		Ditto	,, ,,	,, ,,
,,	William Pitt	Died of his wounds	24 Apr.	—
Surg.	Thomas Rose	To England in charge of sick	June	July
Ast. Sur.	W. Whymper	Leave to England	5 Jan.	—

where the men went into barracks, and the officers were billeted on the inhabitants till the twenty-third of July; the first battalion then quitted the town for Pauliac, a village on the Garonne, whence they were conveyed in large craft to the *Stirling Castle* of seventy-four guns, at the mouth of the river, on board of which they embarked, and arrived at Spithead on the twenty-eighth ; they then marched to Portman-Street barracks.

While the first battalion was engaged in driving the French out of Spain, six companies of the second battalion of the Coldstream had embarked at Greenwich for Holland, under Lieutenant-Colonel Adams, on the twenty-fourth of November, 1813, and landed at Scheveling on the sixth of December, from which place they marched to The Hague, and thence to Delft and Helvoet Sluys. On the sixteenth they embarked and sailed to Williamstadt, and went to Steenbergen, then moved into cantonments near Bergen-op-Zoom, and returned to Steenbergen on the ninth of January, where they were inspected on the twenty-first by His Royal Highness the Duke of Clarence. They passed through Esschen, West Wesel, and continued their route through Rosendale, Staebroeck, to Santvliet, for the purpose of attacking the fortress of Bergen-op-Zoom.

Sir Thomas Graham had collected about four thousand British bayonets to carry this strong fortress by a *coup-de-main*; for which purpose the troops were formed in four columns: two were to attack at different points; the third was to make a false attack; while the fourth attempted the entrance of the harbour, which was fordable at low water.

Major-General Cooke led the left, and met with some impediments from the ice in crossing the ditch, but succeeded in gaining the rampart.

The right column, under Major-General Skerret, forced itself into the town; but that officer being wounded, and great loss sustained, much confusion prevailed.

The centre column, which was driven back, formed again, and advanced to effect a junction with the left column on the ramparts. At daylight the besieged turned the guns on the British, who were without protection on the outworks. General Cooke at length ordered the Guards to retreat, which was conducted in the steadiest and most soldier-like manner.

General Bizanet, the governor of the fortress, agreed to a suspension of hostilities.

The loss of the British amounted to about three hundred killed, and one thousand eight hundred prisoners, amongst whom were many wounded.

The casualties in the Coldstream, during the eighth and ninth of March, were, Captain Shawe, severely wounded; one rank and file killed, and about thirty taken prisoners.

The following is an extract from the Brigade Order;—

Hogerhyde, March 10, 1814.

Colonel Lord Proby returns his best thanks to the officers, non-commissioned officers, and privates of the detachment from the third brigade of Guards who were engaged in the attack upon Bergen-op-Zoom: he feels equally satisfied with the gallantry which they displayed in the assault with their steady conduct during the many hours they maintained their position upon the ramparts; and with the soldierly and orderly manner in which they effected the retreat.

Lord Proby particularly remarked the excellent conduct of the officers who commanded the advanced party, and that which carried the ladders: Captain Rodney, Ensign Gooch, and Ensign Pardoe.

The six companies of the second battalion of the Coldstream were successively quartered at West Wesel, Mechlin, Lippelo, and Dendermonde. They afterwards crossed the Scheld and took possession of Antwerp.

On the third of August they moved to Mechlin, and entered Brussels next day. On the second of September the colours and four companies joined from England, completing the detachment to ten companies.

OFFICERS OF THE SIX COMPANIES OF THE SECOND BATTALION OF THE COLDSTREAM WHO EMBARKED FOR HOLLAND, 24th Nov. 1813.

Present.	From	To	Present.	From	To	Present.	From	To
	1813.	1814.		1813.	1814.		1813.	1814.
Lt. Cl. L.F.Adams	Nov.	Sept.	Capt. W.L.Walton, Acting Adjt.	Nov.	31 Dec.	Ens. J. Mills	Nov.	Feb.
,, H. Loftus	,,	June	,, Thomas Bligh	,,	Sept.	,, T. S. Duncombe	,,	Sept.
			,, Charles Shawe	,,	,,	,, F. Eyre	,,	
			,, John Talbot	,,	,,	,, T. Powys	,,	,,
			,, G. H. Percival	,,	,,	,, H Gooch	,,	31 Dec.
			,, W. G. Baynes	,,	31 Dec.	,, A. Cuyler	,,	,,

		Nov.	Sept.
Adjutant, Capt. C. A. F. Bentinck }		Nov.	Sept.
Acts. Adjt. ,, W. L. Walton		Sept.	31 Dec.
Ast. Surg. ,, George Smith		,,	,,
,, ,, ,, Sept. Worrell		,,	March.

Officers joined		Present.		Officers absent.	Cause of absence.	Absent.	
		From	To			From	To
		1814.	1814.			1814.	1814.
Ens.	M. Beaufoy	{ Jan. Dec.	Oct. 31 Dec.	Capt. John Mills	Leave to England	Feb.	31 Dec.
Lt.-Col.	J. Macdonell	May	Sept.	Ast. Sur. } S. Worrell	{ Ordered to England }	April	,,
Bⁿ.Surg.	W. Whymper	March	31 Dec.	Lt. Cl. Henry Loftus	Leave. To 1st bat.	July	,,
	The remaining companies of the second battalion embarked for Holland 27 Aug. 1814.			,, J. Macdonell	{ Ordered to join 1st bat. }	Sept.	,,
				,, L. F. Adams	Ditto	,,	,,
Col.	H. F. Bouverie	Aug.	31 Dec.	Capt. Thomas Bligh	Ditto	,,	,,
Lt.-Col.	D. Mac Kinnon	,,	. Dec.	,, Charles Shawe	Ditto	,,	,,
,,	Hon. J. Walpole }	,,	31 ,,	,, John Talbot	Ditto	,,	,,
Capt.	E. Sumner	,,	. Dec.	,, G. H. Percival	Ditto	,,	,,
,,	J. L. Blackman	,,	. Dec.	,, C. Shirley	Ditto	,,	,,
,,	W. Grimstead	,,	31 ,,	Ens. T. S. Duncombe }	Ditto	,,	,,
,,	Hon. J. Rous	,,	Oct.	,, Francis Eyre	Ditto	,,	,,
,,	C. Shirley	,,	Sept.	,, Thomas Powys	Ditto	,,	,,
,,	J. Drummond	,,	31 Dec.	Adjut. C.A.F.Bentinck }	{ Dep. Assist. Adjt.-Gen. }	,,	,,
,,	Hon. R. Moore	,,	,,	Capt. Hon. J. Rous	Leave of absence	Oct.	,,
Ens.	H. F. Griffiths	,,	,,	Ens. Mark Beaufoy	Ditto	,,	Nov.
,,	J. F. Buller	,,	,,	,, F. I. Douglas	Ditto	,,	31 Dec.
,,	John Montagu	,,	,,	,, Robert Bowen	Ditto	,,	Nov.
,,	G. R. Buckley	,,	,,	Lt. Cl. D. Mac Kinnon	Ditto	Dec.	31 Dec.
,,	James Hervey	,,	,,	,, W. Gomm	Ditto	,,	,,
,,	Henry Vane	,,	,,	Capt. J. L. Blackman }	Ditto	,,	,,
,,	F. I. Douglas	,,	Oct.				
,,	R. Bowen	{ ,, Dec.	Oct. 31 Dec.				
	A. Gordon	Aug.	,,				
Quʳ. Mʳ.	B. Selway	,,	,,				
AstSurg.	W. Hunter	,,	,,				
Col.	Hon. Alex. Abercromby }	Oct.	,,				
Lt.-Col.	W. Gomm	Nov.	. Dec.				
,,	H. Wyndham	,,	31 ,,				
Capt.	G. Bowles	Oct.	,,				
,,	T. Sowerby	Nov.	,,				
,,	B. Lord Hotham }	,,	,,				

CHAPTER 12

Battle of Waterloo

At the Congress of Vienna in 1815, it was made a question, whether St. Helena should be selected as the place of Napoleon's future residence; the Duke of Wellington opposed the measure, and it was given up. Napoleon, who had been informed that the Allied monarchs had it in contemplation to send him to that remote island, escaped from Elba in a brig, accompanied by three small vessels containing about eleven hundred men, among whom were one hundred dismounted Polish cavalry. On the first of March he landed near Cannes, in the Gulf of Juan, reached Lyons on the tenth, and ten days after made his triumphal entry into Paris, Louis the Eighteenth having fled to Ghent.

A message was delivered to both Houses from the prince regent, declaring his intention to join the Allies.

Austria, Russia, Prussia, and England entered into an agreement not to lay down their arms till Napoleon was again deprived of the supreme power in France. (The expenditure of England during the year 1815 amounted to upwards of one hundred and sixteen millions!)

The Coldstream left Brussels on the twenty-fourth of March for Ath. The Prince of Orange at one time had determined to attack Lille; but this scheme was overruled, and the Guards returned to Enghien.

Reinforcements were almost daily sent from England, all the troops that could be spared were hurried to the Low Countries; even those on their return from America were forwarded without disembarking: the exertions on the part of government were unremitting.

At this period the Duke of Wellington was at Brussels: the right wing of his army in and about Ath was commanded by Lord Hill; the left, in the vicinity of Braine le Comte and Nivelle, was under the Prince of Orange; the Earl of Uxbridge, with the cavalry, was stationed about Grammont; the reserve was in the town and neighbourhood of Brussels. The forces under the Duke of Wellington amounted to seventy-eight thousand five hundred and five men, but the actual number in the field did not exceed sixty-four thousand, with one hundred and twenty guns, including twelve with the reserve. (The Belgians had also forty guns.)

Napoleon quitted Paris on the twelfth, and on the fourteenth he placed himself at the head of his troops, to whom he addressed the following proclamation:—

Avesnes, June 14th

Soldiers!

This day is the anniversary of Marengo and Friedland, which twice decided the destiny of Europe. Then, as after the Battles of Austerlitz and Wagram, we were too generous. We believed in the protestations and oaths of princes, to whom we left their thrones. Now however, leagued together, they strike at the independence and sacred rights of France. They have committed unjust aggressions. Let us march forward and meet them. Are we not still the same men? Soldiers at Jena, these Prussians, now so arrogant, were three to one; at Montmirail six to one. Let those who have been captives to the English describe the nature of their prison-ships, and the sufferings they endured.

The Saxons, the Belgians, the Hanoverians, the soldiers of the Confederation of the Rhine, lament that they are obliged to use their arms in the cause of princes, who are the enemies of justice, and destroyers of the rights of nations. They well know the coalition to be insatiable. After having swallowed up twelve millions of Poles, twelve millions of Italians, one million of Saxons, and six millions of Belgians, they now wish to devour the states of the second order among the Germans. Madmen! one moment of prosperity has bewildered them.

To oppress and humble the people of France is out of their power; once entering our territory, there they will find their doom. Soldiers! we have forced marches before us, battles to fight, and dangers to encounter; but firm in resolution, victory must be ours. The honour and happiness of our country are at stake! and, in short, Frenchmen, the moment is arrived when we must conquer or die!

The French Army of Flanders was composed of nearly twenty thousand men of the Imperial Guard, and five *corps d'armée*, besides a force of about twelve thousand cavalry under Grouchy, and the Young Guards which made, at a moderate calculation, a total of one hundred and fifty thousand men, with two hundred and ninety-six pieces of artillery. During the night of the fifteenth, Wellington obtained information that the enemy had crossed the Sambre, and were marching in force on Charleroi and Fleurus; the troops in their different cantonments received orders to move on Nivelle, where the Prince of Orange was stationed.

The Coldstream left Enghien at three o'clock in the morning of the sixteenth, and, after resting about four hours at Braine le Comte, pushed on to Quatre Bras, where only a small portion of the army was assembled. The division of Guards thus made a march of twenty-five miles. When the Second Brigade halted, the light companies were sent round on the left of the Bois de Bossu, in rear of the Brunswickers.

The Coldstream did not reach the position until about four o'clock in the afternoon; and notwithstanding their fatigue, immediately deployed in support of the First Guards. That brigade was at the time engaged with the enemy, and greatly distinguished itself, though not without suffering severely. After clearing the wood, they retired, and the light companies of the Second Brigade under Lieutenant-Colonel Macdonell took the advance; on his right were detachments from the battalion companies of the Third Guards under Lieutenant-Colonel Home, which communicated with the Brunswickers.

Lieutenant-Colonel Daniel Mackinnon, with four companies, went in support. The troops maintained their ground with firm intrepidity, and repulsed at all points the repeated efforts of a large body of cavalry under Kellerman, who made frequent and desperate charges, seconded by two *corps d'armée* and a considerable preponderance in artillery. At the close of day, the firing ceased. Marshal Ney then rallied on the height of Frasnes. The loss of the Allies amounted to about four thousand men; that of the French to rather more.

The British cavalry and the remainder of the army came up during the night.

While Ney was endeavouring to force the position at Quatre Bras, in which he was unsuccessful, Napoleon attacked and defeated the Prussians at St. Amand and Ligny. During the night, Marshal Blücher, who found himself, after the loss of fifteen thousand men, too weak to retain his position at Sombreff, retired to concentrate on Wavre. It was not till the morning of the seventeenth that the disaster of the Prussians was known at Quatre Bras.

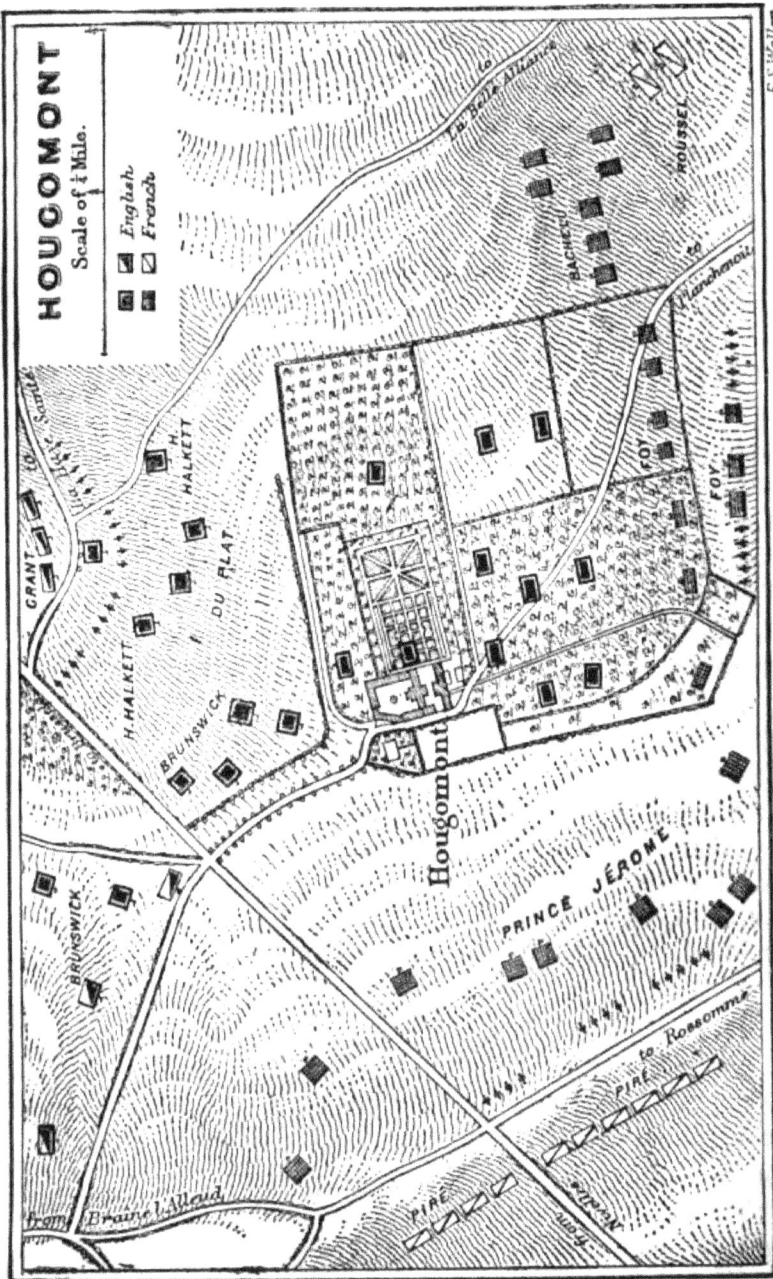

HOUGOMONT
Scale of ¼ Mile.

English
French

to La Belle Alliance

to Plancenoit

BACHELU

ROSSEL

FOY

FOY

GRANT

to Sart a Walhain

H. HALKETT

H. HALKETT

DU PLAT

BRUNSWICK

BRUNSWICK

Hougomont

PRINCE JÉROME

PIRÉ

PIRÉ

to Rossomme

from Braine l'Alleud

F. S. Weller.

Wellington in consequence made a corresponding movement: at ten o'clock his army fell back in perfect order through Genappe on Waterloo. The two light companies of the Second Brigade of Guards, being ordered to mask the retreat on the right, did not leave the ground till past two o'clock,

A body of the enemy's lancers, supported by masses of cavalry, attempted to harass the rear: they were bravely attacked on their advance from Genappe by the Seventh Hussars, who failed, after a gallant effort. Colonel Elley had however taken the precaution to order the First Life Guards to be prepared: that celebrated body of men then charged with the most determined impetuosity, and overthrew the French cavalry. About five p.m. the allied army had taken up its position, which crossed the roads from Nivelle and Charleroi. In front of the Nivelle road was the *château* and garden of Hugomont; fronting the left centre was the farm of La Haye Sainte,

The enemy, with the exception of Marshal Grouchy's corps, detached for the purpose of observing the Prussians, were on the opposite heights: the space between was open, and the two armies were not more than three quarters of a mile from each other; in some places nearer. Before the position was a gentle descent. The Second Brigade of Guards was situated on the right of the centre, and crowned the slope above Hugomont. The *château* of Hugomont faced the enemy without any external fence in its front.

Behind it was the farmyard, protected on the left and rear by a wall, and on the right by farm buildings. To the left of the house and yard was a garden surrounded by a wall, and to the left of that, but adjoining, there was an orchard enclosed by a hedge and ditch, A large gate in the rear led into the yard, and through that supplies were received during the action; two other entrances to the yard were closed up. Outside of the buildings on the right there was a road and a high hedge. A wood in front, which stretched some distance to the right, covered this post. (See plan.)

Although the number of disposable troops under Wellington at the opening of the campaign has been stated at sixty-four thousand, yet, after deducting the corps of observation, which consisted of five thousand men, under Prince Frederick of Orange at Halle, and the four thousand lost at Quatre Bras, the duke's force at Waterloo cannot be rated at more than fifty five thousand.

The army under Napoleon has always been estimated at one hundred and fifty thousand men. Supposing he lost twelve thousand at

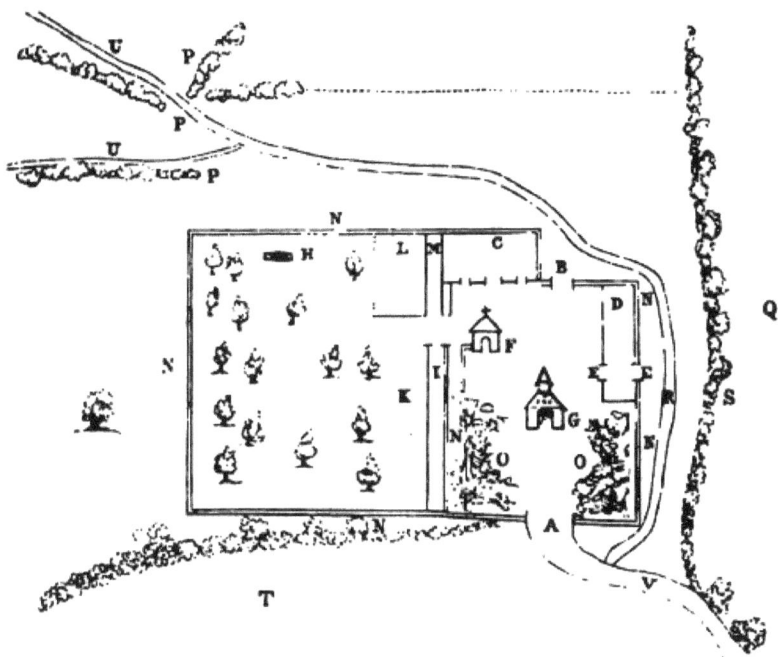

A	Great Gate.
B	Arched Gate.
C	Farm House.
D	Barn.
E	Barn-doors.
F	Chapel.
G	Pigeon-house.
H	Blackman's Tomb.
I	Little Garden.
K	Wood Pales.
L	Vegetable Garden.
M	Garden.
N	Walls separating the Garden from the Orchard, &c.
O	Ruins.
P	Gaps into the Orchard and Fields.
Q	Field leading to Mon Plaisir, where Jerome Buonaparte was.
R	Lane.
S	High Hedge.
T	Hollow Way.
U	Pathways.
V	Lane leading to Nivelle Road.

Ligny, Quatre Bras, and on the seventeenth; allowing also for the corps with Grouchy, which might amount to forty-five thousand, there remains a numerical superiority of at least thirty-eight thousand.

The Battle of Waterloo has been so often described, that it is proposed to confine the narrative as much as possible to those particulars which strictly relate to the part taken in the conflict by the Second Brigade of Guards and the light companies of the First Brigade.

Soon after the Guards reached the position, the light companies were sent to the post of Hugomont.

★★★★★★

The First Brigade of Guards was composed of the second and third battalions of the First Guards, under Major-General Maitland; the Second Brigade, of the second battalion of the Coldstream, and the second battalion of the Third Guards, under Major-General Byng.

★★★★★★

The light companies of the Second Brigade took possession of the orchard for a short time, after which they were placed in the wood; the two light companies of the First Brigade under Lieutenant-Colonel Lord Saltoun then occupied the orchard. The enemy had also despatched a party to the *château*, who, on perceiving the advance of the detachment, made a rush to get first into the place: the two parties came in contact: after an exchange of shots Saltoun secured the post. He was reinforced by three companies of Hanoverian *Yagers*; these men joined the advance piquet under Captain Evelyn and Ensign Standen of the Third Guards.

The light companies of the Second Brigade, composed of the light infantry of the Coldstream under Lieutenant-Colonel Henry Wyndham, and that of the Third under Lieutenant-Colonel Charles Dashwood, covered the right of the *château*. Those of the First Brigade communicated from the orchard with the wood. These companies therefore during the night acted as piquets to the force under Lieutenant-Colonel Macdonell in the *château*, who had been detached with the light companies of the Second Brigade, and on whom, as senior officer, the command devolved. He reached Hugomont about seven in the evening, and, was unceasingly employed in preparing for its defence.

After the brigade had taken up their ground, heavy rain fell, accompanied by wind, lightning, and loud thunder: the position was chiefly covered with standing corn, but the Coldstream occupied a bean-field bearing young crop a few inches high, which soon became knee deep in mire, and every vestige of vegetation disappeared. A recollection of the recent unexpected attack on the Prussians, the proximity of the enemy, the fury of the storm, and the darkness of the night, kept the battalion on the alert till dawn appeared.

On the morning of the eighteenth, as additional means of strengthening the place, loop-holes were made in the building and garden walls of Hugomont. Platforms were also erected, and the gates barricaded, with the exception of one in the rear, which was left open intentionally; these precautions assisted materially in making good the most memorable defence perhaps recorded in the annals of modern warfare.

★★★★★★

A truly characteristic trait of the Duke of Wellington occurred on the morning of the Battle of Waterloo.

General Alava went from Brussels to join his Grace, and found him in a tree observing the movements of the French Army. On the duke turning round and seeing General Alava, be called out, "How are you, Alava? Buonaparte shall see today how a general of *sepoys* can defend a position!"—a remark which showed at once his contempt for an opinion given of him by Buonaparte, and a confidence in himself and in his troops, accompanied with a degree of cheerfulness almost amounting to an assurance of victory.

★★★★★★

Previous to the battle, the Duke of Wellington, attended by his staffs rode through the wood of Hugomont, where he saw Lieutenant-Colonel Macdonell, told him he would be immediately attacked, and gave orders to "defend the post to the last extremity."

At ten o'clock the light companies of the Guards were relieved by a battalion of eight hundred Nassau light troops: part of this corps was stationed in the lofts, buildings, yards; and out-offices; the remainder, with the Hanoverian *Yagers*, were distributed in the orchard and wood. Lord Saltoun then joined the Second Brigade on the position. Lieutenant-Colonel Macdonell with his companies moved to the right of the *château*.

At twenty minutes past eleven o'clock, the first gun was fired from a battery in front of the Second Brigade of Guards; it made a gap for a moment of the head of the column commanded by Prince Jerome Buonaparte, as it moved to the attack on Hugomont.

Outside the south gate, Hougoumont

★★★★★★

About ten o'clock he commenced a furious attack upon our post at Hugomont. I had occupied that post with a detachment from General Byng's brigade of Guards, which was in position in its rear; and it was for some time under the command of Lieutenant-Colonel Macdonell and afterwards of Colonel Home; and I am happy to add that it was maintained throughout with the utmost gallantry by those brave troops, notwithstanding the repeated efforts of large bodies of the enemy to obtain possession of it.—Duke of Wellington's Dispatch. Waterloo, July 19th, 1815.

★★★★★★

The advance of the enemy was covered by a "tremendous cannonade" on the whole line from upwards of two hundred guns.

Shortly after the action had commenced, the *tiralleurs* drove the Nassau battalion and the company of Hanoverian *Yagers* through the wood to the rear of the *château*. This attack was repulsed by the two companies of the Second Brigade. The French were fast closing round, when Macdonell charged and drove them back on their advancing columns. These attempts were vigorously repeated for an hour and a half, but each time they failed.

About one o'clock a cart of ammunition, which had been sent for early in the day, was brought into the farmyard of Hugomont, and proved most seasonable. The men had only time to fill their pouches, when a discharge of artillery suddenly burst upon them, mingled with the shouts of a column rushing on to a fresh attack, A cloud of *tiralleurs* pushed through the wood and cornfields: they were aimed at with fatal certainty from the loopholes, windows, and summit of the building.

But the enemy eventually compelled the few men that remained outside to withdraw into the *château* by the rear gate. In the meantime, the French redoubled their efforts against it, and the fire of the immediate defenders of that point for a moment ceased. The gate was then forced. At this critical moment, Macdonell rushed to the spot with the officers and men nearest at hand, and not only expelled the assailants, but reclosed the gate. The enemy from their overwhelming numbers again entered the yard, when the Guards retired to the house, and kept up from the windows such a destructive fire, that the French were driven out, and the gate once more was closed.

General Foy having chased the Nassau troops before him, passed

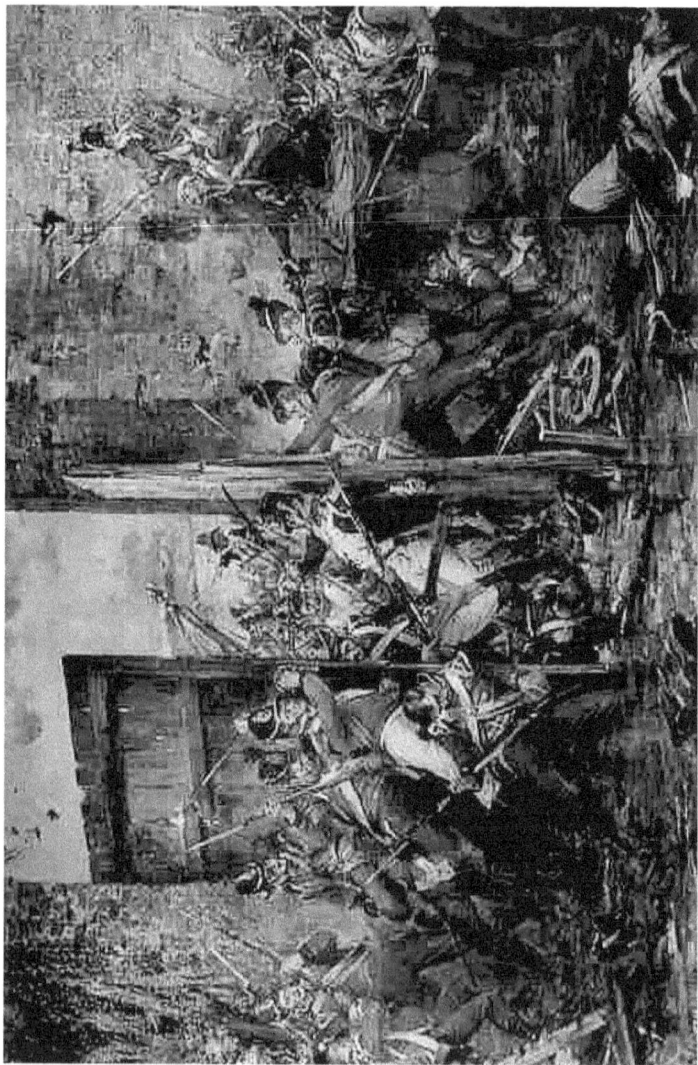

CLOSING NORTH GATES AT HOUGOUMONT

through the wood and surrounded the *château*: all attempts to rally these men proving fruitless, Lieutenant-Colonel Mackinnon with the grenadiers and first company moved to the support of the place, and the enemy were forced back. Lieutenant-Colonel Acheson then joined: the whole followed in pursuit and entered the wood, where they were received with an incessant discharge of small arms.

Colonel Woodford left the seventh and eighth companies in the position for the protection of the colours, and brought down the rest of the battalion. The third and fourth companies of the Third Guards were also sent to Hugomont under Lieutenant-Colonel Home, and occupied the hollow way near the entrance of the wood; these were succeeded by other detachments of equal strength from the same regiment.

On the retreat of the Nassau troops, Lord Saltoun with the light companies of the First Brigade was again ordered to Hugomont, and recovered the orchard, and also part of the wood in its front; the latter, however, there was no possibility of holding in opposition to the vast superiority of the enemy. Lord Saltoun therefore made occasional sallies from the orchard: his orders were, in the event of its being forced to retire into the *château*; but he defended it against every attempt.

The entrance of the wood was attacked in the most gallant manner by the Coldstream. The companies under Colonel Woodford cheered, and after charging, opened a fire, but the powerful resistance they met with could not be overcome. This officer therefore retired, and entered Hugomont.

Afterwards the enemy exerted themselves to carry the orchard. They twice got possession of the hedge, but gained no further ground, as the defenders were firm, and the troops on the garden wall which overlooked the orchard poured in a cross fire and occasioned them severe loss.

A detachment from the Third Guards, and the grenadiers of that corps, with fifty Hanoverian riflemen under Lord Saltoun, bravely charged a howitzer, but did not succeed. This, however, had the effect of stopping anything further on that side, and the enemy contented themselves with firing from behind a ditch which ran nearly parallel to the hedge and ditch in front of the orchard.

At two o'clock. Lord Saltoun was relieved by Lieutenant-Colonel Mercer of the Third Guards, who arrived with reinforcements. The Third Guards had been moved for the purpose of support by detachments of two companies at intervals, and after Colonel Woodford

THE FRENCH ATTACK THE SOUTH GATE, HOUGOUMONT

THE NORTH GATE AT HOUGOUMONT AFTER THE ATTACK

entered Hugomont with the Coldstream, they occupied the orchard, under Colonel Hepburn.

The enemy were undaunted in their attacks; but Hugomont was defended with a calm and stubborn gallantry, that alone could have enabled so small a force to resist the repeated and fierce assaults of nearly thirty thousand men, of whom the second French corps was composed. The cross discharge from the artillery was incessant: the bursting of shells set part of the building in flames, and as the fire extended to the chapel and stables, many of the wounded soldiers of the Coldstream perished.

The Guards, nevertheless, at no time exceeding two thousand men, maintained the post amidst the terrible conflagration within, and the murderous fire of the enemy from without. (Exclusive of the eight hundred Nassau light troops and three companies of Hanoverian riflemen.) When the contention terminated, the French dead lay piled round the *château*, in the wood, and every avenue leading to it.

> *The Field of Waterloo (Chapter 23)*
> *Farewell, sad Field! whose blighted face*
> *Wears desolation's withering trace;*
> *Long shall my memory retain*
> *Thy shatter'd huts and tramped grain.*
> *With every mark of martial wrong.*
> *That scathe thy towers, fair Hugomont!*
> *Yet though thy gardenia green arcade*
> *The marksman's fatal post was made;*
> *Though on thy shatter'd beeches fell*
> *The blended rage of shot and shell;*
> *Though from thy blacken'd portals torn.*
> *Their fall thy blighted fruit-trees mourn,*
> *Has not such havock brought a name*
> *Immortal in the rolls of fame?*
> *Yes,—Agincourt may be forgot,*
> *And Cressy be an unknown spot.*
> *And Blenheim's name be new;*
> *But still in story and in song,*
> *For many an age remember'd long,*
> *Shall live the towers of Hugomont*
> *And field of Waterloo.*
> Walter Scott.

BATTLE OF WATERLOO
June 18th, 1815.
7.45 p.m.

Scale of 1 Mile

REFERENCE
Allies — Prussians — French

LIST OF KILLED AND WOUNDED IN THE SECOND BRIGADE OF GUARDS, INCLUDING THE LIGHT COMPANIES OF THE FIRST BRIGADE.

FIRST REGIMENT OF FOOT GUARDS.
OFFICERS PRESENT AT THE BATTLE OF WATERLOO.

Company.	Rank.	Names	Remarks.	Company.	Rank.	Names.	Remarks.
Light Company, 2ᵈ Bat.	Lt.-Col. Capt. ,, Ensign	W. H. Milne T. Brown F. F. Luttrell A. Greville	Killed. Wounded.	Light Company, 3ᵈ Bat.	Lt.-Col. Capt. ,,	Lord Saltoun Ed. Grose C. P. Ellis	Commanding. Wounded.

Grenadier Guards Orderly-Room.

COLDSTREAM GUARDS.
OFFICERS PRESENT AT THE BATTLE OF WATERLOO.

Company.	Rank.	Names.	Remarks.	Company.	Rank.	Names.	Remarks.
Grenadier	Colonel	A. Woodford	Commands. the batta.	Fourth	Lt.-Col. Capt. Ensign	Hon.E.Acheson J. L. Blackman A. Gordon	Killed.
	Lt.-Col.	D. MacKinnon	Wounded. Acting 2nd Major. Died of his wounds, 26 June.	Fifth	Ensign ,, ,,	R. Bowen J. F. Douglas C. Short	
	Capt.	E. Sumner					
	Ensign	H. F. Griffiths	Wounded.	Sixth	Lt.-Col. Capt.	H. Wyndham Lord Hotham.	Wounded.
First	Lt.-Col.	J. Macdonell	Actg. 1st Maj. Detached to Hugomont.	Seventh	Capt. Ensign	G. Bowles J. Hervey	
	Capt.	T Sowerby					
	Ensign	I. Montagu	Wounded.	Eighth	Lt.-Col. Ensign	H. Dawkins M. Beaufoy	
Second	Colonel	Hon.A.Abercrombie	Assist. Qur.-Mar.-Genl.	Light Infantry	Capt. ,, Ensign	W. L. Walton Hon. R. Moore H. Gooch	Actg. Adjutant. Wounded.
	Ensign	Hon. J. Forbes					
	,,	A. Cuyler	Staff.				
Third	Lt.-Col.	Sir W. Gomm	Staff.	Staff	Adjut. Capt. }	A. F. Bentinck	D.A.Adj.Genl.
	Capt.	T. S. Cowell	Taken sick evening of 17th, went to Brussels.		Qur. Mr.	B. Selway	
					Surgeon	W. Whymper	
	Ensign	H. Vane	Wounded.		Asst. Surt. }	George Smith	
	,,	Hon.W.Forbes			,, ,,	W. Hunter	
				1st Bat.	Lt.-Col.	Freemantle	Staff.

Coldstream Orderly-Room.

THIRD REGIMENT OF FOOT GUARDS.
OFFICERS PRESENT AT THE BATTLE OF WATERLOO.

Company.	Rank.	Names.	Remarks.	Company.	Rank.	Names.	Remarks.
Grenadiers	Colonel	F. Hepburn	{ Commands. the batts.	Seventh	Lt.-Col.	Hon. Sir A. Gordon	Killed. (A. D. C. to Com. of the Forces.)
	Lt.-Col.	F. Home	Actg. 2nd Maj.		Capt.	Hon. H. Forbes	Killed.
	Capt.	R. B. Hesketh	Wounded.		,,	R. H. Wigston	On guard at Waterloo.
	,,	John Ashton	Killed.		Ensign	Charles Lake	Wounded.
First	Lt.-Col.	E. Bowater	Wounded.		,,	David Baird	Wounded.
	Capt.	T. Crawford	Killed.	Eighth	Lt.-Col.	Charles West	Wounded.
	Ensign	B. Drummond	Acting Adjut.		Capt.	Montgomerie	Wounded.
	,,	H. S. Blane			Ensign	I. Prendergast	
Second	Capt.	H. Hawkins			,,	H. B. Montagu	
	Ensign	W. James	BaggageGuard.	Light Infantry	Lt.-Col.	C. Dashwood	Wounded.
	,,	W.F. Hamilton			Capt.	G. Evelyn	Wounded.
Third	Lt.-Col.	D. Mercer	Actg. 1st Maj.		,,	John Elrington	
	Capt.	C. J. Barnett			Ensign	G. D. Standen	
	Ensign	W. Butler		Staff	Adjut.	W. Stothert	Killed. (Brig.-Maj. to 2nd Brig. of Guards.)
Fourth	Capt.	B. Drummond			Qur. Mr.	J. Skuce	
	Ensign	Simpson	Killed.		Surgeon	S. Good	
Fifth	Lt.-Col.	C. F. Canning	Killed. (A. D. C. to Com. of the Forces.)		Asst. Surt.	F. G. Hanrott	
	Capt.	E. B. Fairfield			,, ,,	J. R. Ward	
	Ensign	T. Wedgwood					
	,,	A.C. Cochrane					
Sixth	Lt.-Col.	H. W. Rooke	Asst. A.Genl. 1st Division.				
	Capt.	J. W. Moorhouse					
	Ensign	Hon.E.Stopford	A. D. C. to Maj.-Genl. Sir J. Byng.				
	,,	Hon. G. Anson	On guard in the village of Waterloo.				

Scots Fusilier Guards Orderly-Room.

RETURN OF KILLED, WOUNDED, AND MISSING, ON THE 18th OF JUNE, 1815

	Capts.	Lieuts.	Ensigns.	Serjts.	Drumrs.	Rank and file.
Second Battalion, Coldstream Guards, killed	,,	1	,,	1	,,	33
wounded *	2	2	3	13	,,	229
missing	,,	,,	,,	,,	1	3
Second Battalion, Third Guards, killed	,,	3	,,	2	,,	37
wounded †	,,	3	3	10	,,	178

—London Gazette, 8th July, 1815.

* Died of their wounds, 1 Lieutenant, 1 serjeant, 27 rank and file.

† Died of their wounds, 3 serjeants, 3 corporals, 41 rank and file.

The loss of the two light companies of the second and third battalions of the First Guards is included in the returns of their respective battalions.

★★★★★★

The following is an extract from the Duke of Wellington's dispatch:

> It gives me the greatest satisfaction to assure your lordship that the army never upon any occasion conducted itself better. The division of Guards under Lieutenant-General Cooke, who is severely wounded, Major-General Maitland, and Major-General Byng, set an example which was followed by all.

Silver medals were given to every officer and soldier present during the sixteenth, seventeenth, and eighteenth.

★★★★★★

Waterloo exemplifies in a high degree that obstinate and determined courage under fire which the troops of Great Britain had attained in the school of Wellington. In giving some account of this battle as far as the Guards were concerned, the writer has had the gratification of concluding his work by exhibiting the part taken by them in that memorable conflict.

The state of Europe at that time is well known. The policy of Wellington was to act on the defensive, not to seek an action, nor yet to retreat before Napoleon, A million of bayonets were advancing from all parts of the Continent to put down his newly-resumed power; but they were not yet all assembled. The scheme of the emperor was to attack and defeat in detail the several armies by which he was to be opposed. The French were sufficiently powerful to justify such an expectation. The Prussians, overthrown on the sixteenth of June, had retired in disorder.

The next and most important object of Napoleon was the destruction of the English: this completed, the other armies might be panic-struck, and the confederacy against France dissolved. The Belgians detested the Dutch connexion, and the Russians being paralysed, the Emperor of Austria, finding the scale of chances balanced, was not unlikely to declare for his son-in-law. Had these events taken place,

France no longer checked, and the star of Napoleon regaining the ascendant, the liberties of Europe would once more have been sampled under the feet of his victorious legions. Such were the natural anticipations of the French, should they triumph. The struggle, therefore, with the English was not one of common occurrence; the contest was for supremacy, for glory, for everything held most dear by the gallant and chivalrous troops of France.

The enemy chose his ground, his time, and mode of attack; his troops were far more numerous, and were animated by their recent victory over the veteran Blücher.

To ensure success, the energies and experience of the great and comprehensive mind of Napoleon were concentrated. The recollections of the rivalship of the two nations, of their military predominance in Europe, of soldiers raised to the rank of generals and afterwards to thrones, were revived in the French Army, by all those arts, the practice of which, a long and intimate acquaintance with the French character had taught Napoleon. He called on his veterans to conquer, and told them the day was arrived for retrieving the disasters of the Russian campaign of Dresden, Leipsic, Montmartre, and Paris.

The emperor called not in vain; promotion, pillage, and revenge dashed before the ardent and inflamed imaginations of the French soldiery. The triumphs of Marengo and Austerlitz animated them with hope; their former conquests, their valour, their numbers, and the well-known talents of their chief, made them feel secure of victory. Every soldier in the Imperial Army was sensible of the importance of the day: Napoleon took advantage of their enthusiasm, and with infinite skill made his preparations.

The advance of the French at Waterloo was covered by an immense artillery; their native courage was heightened by every sentiment that can stimulate the human breast.

Wellington, aware of the enemy with whom he had to contend, was also well acquainted with the quality of his own troops, and relied on their cool and steady bravery. He baffled throughout the day the repeated attacks of the French cavalry and infantry. His right was thrown back on a ravine near Merke Braine; on the left his communication with Marshal Blücher at Wavre was open through Ohaine.

The French columns rushed on, supported by their splendid cavalry; the Imperial Guard being in reserve. Their numbers and the renown of their emperor gave a vigour to their movements, not easy to be withstood.

After many severe repulses, Napoleon thought the moment had arrived to throw in his reserve and decide the day; a manoeuvre by which he had so often triumphed over his opponents. His Imperial Guards were ordered to advance and charge the British squares. Labedoyere flew to the fronts exclaiming, "*Courage, mes enfans!* the English waver, and will give way, charge those squares, and the day is ours!" The bullets of the hitherto invincible Imperial Guard whistled through the British ranks, and the French cavalry charged with the determination of men accustomed to vanquish. After heroic deeds had been performed by the Imperial Guard, these fine troops, the first soldiers of the European Continent, remained on the field, a monument of their desperate valour and of the futility of their attempts to shake the impenetrable battalions opposed to them.

★★★★★★

"*Nous les avons vus, au jour de notre désastre, ces enfans d'Albion, formés bataillons carrés dans la plaine entre le bois d'Hougoumont et le village de Mont Saint-Jean. Ils avaient, pour arriver à cette formation compacte, doublé et redoublé leurs rangs à plusieurs reprises. La cavalerie qui les appuyait fut taillée en pieces, le feu de leur arlillerie fut éteint. Les officiers-généraux et d'état-major galopaient d'un carré à l'autre, incertains où ils trouveraient un abri: chariots, blessés, parcs de réserve, troupes auxiliares fuyaient à la débandade vers Bruxelles. La mort était devant eux et dans leurs rangs; la honte derrière. En cette terrible occurrence, les boulets de la Garde Impériale, lancés à brûle-pourpoint, et la cavalerie de France victorieuse, ne purent pas entamer l'immobile infanterie Britannique. On eût été tenté de croire qu'elle avait pris racine dans la terre, si ses bataillons ne se fussent ébranlés majestueusemient quelques minutes après le coucher du soleil, alors que l'arrivée de l'armée Prussienne apprit à Wellington que, grâces au nombre, grâces à la force d'inertie, et pour prix d'avoir su ranger de braves gens en bataille, il venait de remporter la victoire la plus décisive de notre âge.*"—Histoire de la Guerre de la Péninsue sous Napoléon; par le Général Foy, Vol. 1.

Napoleon said, "Even the Old Guard could make no impression on them: their fire was dreadful; and, as to charging, you might as well charge stone walls."

"*La gloire de l'armée Britannique lui vient avant tout de son excellente discipline, et de la bravoure calme et franche de la nation.*"—General Foy vol. 1.

★★★★★★

Then it was that Wellington ordered the line of infantry to advance, and instantly the immoveable British squares that had stood firm as their native rocks, insensible to bullets, to charges of cavalry, and to death, insensible to everything but their duty, moved forward, driving the enemy before them with all the attendant consequences of panic, confusion, and irretrievable ruin.

In other battles, positions have been selected with judgment, and defended with courage; but the strong entrenchments at Genappe were carried by the French levies under Dumourier, and the redoubts of Borodino were insufficient to stop the advance of Napoleon on the ancient capital of the *Czars*, At Waterloo there were no works of military art to cover the British Army. They had, and required no protection but their arms, nor any shelter but their matchless discipline, to enable them to repel the furious assaults of an enemy bent on forcing their position. Their unflinching resistance at first perplexed the scientific calculations of the emperor, then changed his confidence into anxiety, and finally drove him to that state of desperation which flies to a last great effort as its only hope. He had promised victory to his soldiers; he threw his veterans forward, and failed.

Up to this period a large and well-earned portion of the glories of the strife must be given to the brave men who for so many successive hours beat off the attacks of their opponents. Their conduct is beyond all praise, and the merit was their own. But the master-mind that ruled the fight throughout the day, the eagle glance that at its close converted a well-sustained defence into an irresistible charge on the assailing columns and swept them from the ground on which they stood, belonged exclusively to Wellington. He closed on his adversary, and broke the Imperial Sceptre forever.

Thus, was the Battle of Waterloo gained; the most important in its results of ancient or modern times. Here the two greatest captains of this or any other age were opposed to each other: here they were fairly matched, and ample opportunity was afforded for a trial of generalship and military skill. The best troops of France were in the field, and the result is decisive of the superiority of Wellington over his great competitor, while it affords another instance of the unequalled steadiness, perseverance, and courage of the British soldier.

HUGOMONT

www.ingramcontent.com/pod-product-compliance
Lightning Source LLC
Chambersburg PA
CBHW021106090426
42738CB00006B/521